A Week of Awakening

A Practical Guide to Personal Transformation

Dr. Jorge Partida

THIS BOOK IS DEDICATED:

To the memory of all my grandparents –
the Partida's and the Del Toro's;

To my parents, Isidro and Maria Partida Del Toro;
I am grateful for all your sacrifices, most importantly for
risking it all in order to give your children a chance at a future;

To my brothers Luis and Francisco,
as the youngest and first brothers to come to the United States,
I am proud of you and of the parents that you have become;

To Lidia, Carlos and Isidro;
may you never let sadness impede your path to greatness.

Your lives are a story of love and endurance;
a miracle of survival and perseverance.

This book is also dedicated to anyone and everyone that
has ever felt discouraged by the circumstances of their life.
Know that the pain and suffering that you have endured
could never be strong enough to ever keep you down.
Your pain of yesterday is the path to your transformation today.
You have the power within you to transform your life
and to live your promise.

Behold!

Thou hast become the light,

thou hast become the sound,

thou art thy Master and thy God.

Thou art Thyself the object of thy search:

the VOICE unbroken,

that resounds throughout eternities,

exempt from change, from sin exempt,

the seven sounds in one,

THE VOICE OF THE SILENCE.

– The Book of the Golden Precepts

TABLE OF CONTENTS

ACKNOWLEDGEMENTS

I wish to express my deepest and most sincere gratitude to Da'Mon Vann who, for years, has been a solid and consistent source of support with this book and with my first book, "The Promise of the Fifth Sun." Thank you for your invaluable contributions, your keen insights and encouragement. You have taught me much about love, friendship and all that is good in life. Words could never express the depth of my gratitude.

Thanks to Sven Erlandson who has dedicated many long hours to editing this book and has offered his friendship and strength.

I wish to also thank Harini Riana for her friendship and her willingness to always say "yes".

Thanks also to Tracy Dean for her instant and enthusiastic willingness to add her design magic to the cover and lay out of this book.

You are all my family and my support. I appreciate and love you.

INTRODUCTION

Do you sometimes feel as though you are going through life largely asleep? Do you have an undeniable sense that something great is within you, but the heaviness of your pain, responsibilities, fears and suffering can't allow you access to your power? For many people, life has become drudgery; an experience to tolerate rather than enjoy.

We become trapped by the bad news, the failed economy, and the constant threat of annihilation. It seems that, no matter what we do, we feel that we cannot find our success or even any meaning and purpose to life. We focus on the troubles we experience as we try to succeed, make things happen, search for happiness or find true love. Many people have learned to live their lives as if the world is forever trying to keep them suppressed in a constant state of fear. They live with the terrible feeling that something is constantly wrong. So they are in constant pursuit, running to hang on to some fleeting sense of security.

We are all influenced and impacted by so much information that travels through the airwaves and through the internet. Our brains can process information very fast, but they cannot process faster than the rate of stimulation from all the information being released into the atmosphere. Politics, religion and pop culture compete as platforms grabbing at our attention, demanding that we suspend critical thought and accept the irrationality of what we witness. Soon, it seems impossible to distinguish the sound of our own voice from the noise and static that steal our attention and fuel our need for constant consumption. We come to believe we have no power and that we are helpless to transform ourselves, not to mention the world around us.

Changing Our Patterns

We must always strive to stay awake and to be critical thinkers. Thinking critically sometimes means having to swim against the tides of bombardment. No wonder we may sometimes choose to surrender. It seems so much easier to just follow someone that tells us what to think and where to go. Many people prefer to be directed, even if often the messages we consume are filled with fear, lack and limitation. If we are not watchful and awake, we begin to believe that our lives are indeed miserable and restricted. We can become so afraid of change that any idea that pushes our comfort zone becomes a potential threat. Therefore, we continue living restricted lives, afraid of changing and afraid of being the magnificent beings we are intended to be.

At some point or another in our lives, we have all experienced fear of change. Some of us are more afraid than others, but all of us have been dominated by fear. This sense of fear is the engine that drives our 'ego,' which is our sense of individuality and separation. We fear death because we see it as a loss of our uniqueness and individuality. Yet, we cannot deny that change is a universal truth and a constant force of life. Change is the language of evolution and this evolution occurs most rapidly at times when an old cycle or paradigm begins to fall apart while a new order emerges.

We are living through radical transformations in our economy, politics, environment, technology and religion. We are living in the greatest, most powerful era of change and transition. The shifts we experience seem very frightening and leave us feeling uncertain and stressed. To appreciate the rapid rate of change occurring, all we need to do is look around us. The evidence of this shift in consciousness is everywhere.

As a psychologist in private and public practices, I have had the privilege of being on television and radio in the Latino communities of California, Chicago, Mexico, Miami, and South America. I have worked in Africa, Europe, and Latin America. In the many years of my clinical work, I have come to see one very strong pattern emerge in the lives of not only my clients, but also entire communities. *Many people have fallen asleep.* They are living in fear and are dissatisfied with their lives, but are unsure of how to go about making changes. They are going through life as if they were on automatic pilot, unable to see the infinite joy and possibilities that are constantly unfolding before them.

Their lives have become dark and endless nightmares, full of resentments, endless responsibilities, and disappointments. These dark and numbing forces tend to weigh us down and can seem overwhelming. The many critical voices and pressures to which we respond can start when we are young and they can last well into our old age. But that does not have to be. We can have the courage to recognize, confront and remove the negative influences and replace them with more life-giving positive thoughts and beliefs about ourselves and about life itself.

I have seen it in my own life. I have often been told by other people what I could and could not do. Seldom, however, have I allowed these opinions to limit my continued effort and drive to keep moving in the direction of my intended path. From childhood, I learned that I was a sinner, a criminal – a border-crosser without a heritage or a future. At school, teachers always insisted on foretelling my destiny. In grade school, I was labeled "Mildly Mentally Retarded" simply because I did not speak English. Before graduating from high school, the career counselor said I would only be able to aspire as high as being a mechanic (which is an honorable profession, to be sure, but the counselor tried to use it as an insult, as a way to tell me I was not very smart and had limited potential). After graduating from college, a professor told me I did not have the intellect or academic rigor to complete a graduate degree. When I was the head of a doctorate program at a university, I was told my program would never be accredited and I would never be published.

My point is simply this: *You can confront any opinion that tries to limit your worth; any critical voice that would tear you down rather than build you up; and anybody who offers a view that limits your worth. To be truly alive, truly AWAKE, truly happy, you must value your worth, love who you are, and protect your spirit, as a gardener protects young seedlings from the elements that might crush the awakening buds.*

WAKE UP!

If you are feeling stuck, hurt or afraid, you are experiencing a block to your full awakening. With a bit of work, these blocks can be removed and you will have all you need to AWAKEN to the infinite potential that is your life. I know this for fact. I have seen it. I have helped many people reach a point where they have dared to cross the threshold into their AWAKENED life. Your new life is waiting for you, if you are willing to begin the journey.

Understanding the force and source of self-awareness has been the primary interest of our human condition from the beginning of recorded history right down to the present time. The ability to think and reason is what most defines our condition and differentiates humans from any other species. The native Nican-Tlaca tribes, the indigenous groups of civilizations that inhabited the lands we now call the Americas, studied the invisible force of creation. They copied the stars and constellations and duplicated their patterns on earth in the form of pyramids and grand cities so that all could live surrounded by the heavenly movement and rhythm of creation. They believed that life is eternal awareness and consciousness forever expanding. Our ancestors considered life to be an infinite and diverse expression populated by divine embodied beings. They taught us that individuals do not die. We all just evolve into a higher form of awareness. All of us are on this earth as travelers on a journey of self-discovery.

Although for some the journey can be joyful and easy, for others the journey may seem painful, dangerous and long. Our individual souls are on earth, collecting evidence and experiences to be used for the journey of self-realization and transformation. We are all marching in the same direction forever evolving closer to perfection. Ultimately and eventually, we will all reach our final destination and pour ourselves like drops of water into the vast ocean – into the infinite and eternal, unbounded heart of our CREATOR.

Human thought and awareness represent an infinite and ever-evolving field of creation and perception that, like the universe we inhabit, keep expanding in every direction. Your reality is made up entirely of your thoughts, memories and perceptions. Your memories and experiences are projected outward and become the reality you see. Nevertheless, sometimes, your reactions to the world and to people can become doubt-filled, fearful and rigid with constant repetition. When this happens, you may not always be able to maintain an alert and awakened focus to all that is truly unfolding before you. The pull of the past and the uncertainty of the future can leave you feeling as though you are constantly looking back or anxiously peering forward fearing what may happen.

For more than twenty-five thousand years, our ancestors collected their teachings and carefully passed on their knowledge from one generation to the next. Unfortunately, most of their books and texts were destroyed during the arrival of Conquistadores in the New World. The rich heritage and teachings of the Nican-Tlaca represents the most truly American ancient teachings that we have. These teachings are also a part of the collective unconscious of every person on earth. Thus, the legacy of the native healers, scientists, priests and warriors still survives, passed on orally from one generation to the next. This rich field of knowledge belongs to everyone equally, since we are all sons and daughters of the same CREATOR.

Although we no longer have access to the countless books they wrote, we still have access to the central core of ancestral teachings. Our ancestors taught that the most reliable source of knowledge is what we call 'intuitive knowing' and the source of this knowing can be found directly within you. At the center of your being is the voice of your intuition. This is the voice of your higher self, seeking to guide you and to use you as a vehicle of divine expression. This intelligence and loving guidance is ever-present. No matter what has taken place in your life or how much suffering you have endured, you can still access this infinite source of wisdom and power.

Within this book is a powerful message that has survived for thousands of years. It has withstood the tests of time. The wisdom, power and grace of the past can become your anchor as you navigate and explore the ancient art of awakening. This book will show you how you can employ the same healing and transformative practices of awakening used since ancient times. If you apply these easy practices consistently, you will discover your own pathway. You will learn how to tap into the infinite power of your mind. You will find the meaning you seek and you will join your *tonalli* – your 'life potential,' in the words of our ancestors – to the great mystery of creation. Like our ancestors before us, you can learn to understand the cycles of life and unlock the great mysteries. If you learn to release and cultivate the seed of creation, you can make anything happen in your own life.

To AWAKEN you have to be willing to let go of the notion you once held of who and what you were. This letting go can be difficult and disorienting. Even people who have suffered greatly have trouble letting go of their old identity once they recognize they have to change their perception of who they thought they were. Many people prefer to hold on to a limiting sense of reality, because that reality provides a sense of security, even if that sense of security is false. Although so many people say they want to be happy, they also want the familiar comfort of the past and none of the uncertainty that comes with change. The program outlined in this book will work for you, but you must remain open to change and to what reveals itself as you perform the work outlined. These revelations will sometimes be hard to process, but be brave!

You cannot be a better person without facing those thoughts, actions and behaviors that contributed to your pain and suffering. When you remain open to all that reveals itself, sometimes the revelations will sting. However, as you learn to adjust to the truth revealed, you will find that you are slowly uncovering layers to your true self. The more you become acquainted with this higher self, the more you will become convinced that you are capable of greater things than you ever imagined.

As you move forward, remain open to looking at things you have never considered, and remain open to confronting your greatest fears.

There are three steps required to stay open:

1. Maintain an open and receptive attitude;

2. Be willing to let go of your attachment to the past and your need to see reality only according to your expectations;

3. Be willing to adopt the curious perspective of a discoverer and a critical thinker.

If you follow these simple recommendations for staying open, you will discover that this book brings you to new heights of self-awareness, greater personal joy and power. You will begin to live your life guided by purpose and personal fulfillment. With this book you will move into the knowing and living of the path intended for you.

Remember This

The Infinite Mind saw fit to breathe life into you. Never has there been anyone just like you and never again will there ever be another you. You are here in this particular space and time to contribute your wisdom, your power, your strength, your uniqueness, and your truth. The world waits for your critical contribution. How will you contribute? To contribute something new, you have to first AWAKEN to your individuality.

You must discover your truest SELF and recognize that it has been waiting patiently, deep within you, for the invitation to blossom. Your time is now. It is time to claim your ancestral promise and AWAKEN to the light of a new sun, a new awareness of yourself as a divine creation and a co-creator.

1

LEARNING YOUR STORY

¿Aprende agradecer las caídas de la vida.
Si el camino fuera siempre parejo,
no te serviría para crecer."[1]

...Grandmother Lidia

I was seven years old the last time I ever slept soundly.

My sleep habits forever changed on one bitter cold December
night in 1974. I had been fast asleep in my room but began to
stir, restlessly attempting to wrench myself from the snares of
a nightmare. I tried to force my eyes open and yell to awaken
myself, but could not pull out of it, until I felt my Grandmother
Lidia shaking me and whispering in my ear, *"Despierta!*
Despierta!"[2]

---

1   *"Learn to be grateful for life's falls. If the path were always*
    smooth, it would not serve you for your growth."
2   *"Wake up! Wake up!"*

I sat up straight in bed. The room was consumed in darkness as I reassured myself that it was only a bad nightmare, and that nothing was wrong in real life.

My grandmother Lidia had moved more than a year before to live in the United States with her husband and sons. I was still deeply connected to her in very powerful ways. In addition to her frequent letters with dollar bills wrapped in the silver foil paper from her empty cigarette packs, my Grandmother Lidia frequently came to me in my dreams. She would even awaken me from nightmares, just as she did that early morning.

I put my hands to my chest and felt my heart beating fast. But the fears of my nightmare quickly gave way to something worse as my ears focused on the shuffling of feet and muttered whispers that came from our living room. I thought that we were being robbed!

Trying to keep my heart from exploding in my chest, I felt around the darkness for something to use to defend myself and found only my first grade history book. I made my way to the bedroom door and cracked it open as light from the living room poured into the darkened bedroom. Peeking through the door, my eyes began to adjust to the changing light. Although I was able to see into the living room, I could not make sense of what was happening.

Like pieces of some surreal puzzle, images flooded my mind without forming a logical meaning. There were suitcases resting on the ceramic floor. My maternal grandparents, my Aunts Luz

Maria and Virginia were crying quietly into tissues. Perhaps most disturbing, I saw my father crying.

That's strange, I thought! *Why would Papa be crying?*

Then the history book I held above my head fell to the floor with a loud thud as the pieces of the puzzle instantly fell in place. Still it seemed that my brain resisted accepting what my gut perceived. Dread washed over my body and my heart sank through my sickened stomach. I realized suddenly that my parents were leaving and were not planning on saying goodbye or taking us with them.

Mama and Papa were sneaking away like criminals into the darkness of that cold December morning. I screamed louder than I ever had, piercing the hushed quiet of the house. I felt as though the flesh was being stripped away from my bones. I cried out in sheer terror and protest as I ran into the living room. I was suddenly snagged by my aunt, even as my shrieks got louder. My cries woke the other children – my brothers and sisters – who came rushing to grab on to my mom and dad, begging to be taken with.

Mama stood still as her eyes caught mine. I can still see her. An image that has never left my mind. Ever. In one arm, she carried my newborn brother, Luis, who was covered in blankets from head to foot. Her tears landed on his little face, causing him to cry out as if afraid of drowning. Standing like a scared little soldier by her side, my brother Francisco, who was a year and a half old, wrapped his hand around my mother's fingers. His eyes were opened wide in fear and confusion.

My mother and father were leaving for the United States and they were taking the youngest two of their six children. I, the oldest, was being left behind with the other three, including my sister Lidia, and brothers Carlos and Chilo. We would be separated, not only from my mother and father and two youngest brothers, but also from each other. The four of us that remained would each be sent to live with a different relative.

I was seven years old!

"Don't look back! Your children will be fine. Go now, so that you can make good time

to the border," my grandfather, Chemo, yelled out, as I kicked and screamed in protest,

trying to break free from my aunt's tight grip on my arms. I struggled and fought until I broke loose and ran towards the red Camaro that sped away. I chased after the car as fast as my legs would carry me.

It was no use.

The Camaro disappeared behind a cloud of dust and I fell to the ground, wailing. Devastated. Right there, on the ground, my entire life fell apart as the sharp cobblestones cut into my hands. Just like that, my parents and two youngest brothers were gone. The energy and spirit of my Grandmother Lidia had awakened me to witness a child's greatest horror, the loss of his parents. I would forever have etched in my memory the final glimpse of my parents as they left to a different country while my world ended.

As a child, I would never again see my parents on Mexican soil.

Screams of despair rose from the four of us that remained, as we struggled to understand why we had been abandoned by our parents. But before we could even comfort each other, we were instantly separated. I was taken to live with my aunt Virginia in the suburbs of Guadalajara. My sister Lidia and brother Carlos stayed with my maternal grandmother, Juana. My brother, Chilo, was taken to live with my mom's oldest sister, Luz Maria.

The Hopes of an Abandoned Boy

I lived with my Aunt Virginia and Uncle Victor for almost two years, separated from my parents and brothers. During that time, my mother wrote to me almost weekly. I came to live for those letters filled with hope, assurances of love, and promises of someday being reunited once again as a family. I would read the letters over and over, putting them to my nose, trying to catch even the slightest scent of my mother's perfume as evidence that she had held that paper in her own hands.

I would close my eyes to imagine my parents and two youngest brothers living in the famous land of dreams – America. Once, in one of the much anticipated letters, I received a picture of my father, handsome and proud, standing like a soldier with his hands flat to the sides. My mother stood between my two little brothers. Luis, now walking, held a plastic horse in his hands and Francisco looked straight ahead with his big dark eyes. I carried

that picture wherever I went. That picture was my connection
to my family and to the promised lands of *El Norte*.

The time I lived with my Aunt Virginia was very difficult.
She had been recently married to my uncle Victor and was now
pregnant with their first child. It is understandable that she was
nesting and would want to have the small one-bedroom apartment
for her family. One night, I overheard my aunt crying and
complaining about my living with them. I felt so unwanted.

The next day, I decided that I was going to run away, traveling
north to find my parents. I skipped school, found the old *Central
Camionera,*[3] and stole away in one of the three star buses headed
to Ciudad Juarez. The fat bus driver was busy eating his *torta*[4]
away from the vehicle. The door of the bus was left open. I
snuck inside the bus and rolled myself up in a ball under the
last seats in the back.

I could hear other people getting onto the bus. The driver and
the ticket collector got on the bus. The bus rolled slowly out of
the station. Guadalajara was left behind in a cloud of exhaust and
memories. I lay still, rolled in a ball for more than an hour and
a half, until I felt that we were far enough away for me to crawl
out. Slowly, I peeked out and began to emerge from under the
seats. A couple of people sitting nearby looked at me, but no one
said anything. I smiled and sat in an empty seat.

---

3   *Central bus station.*
4   *Mexican sandwich.*

The bus came to a stop in the middle of the road and a couple got on. They sat in the back of the bus, next to where I was sitting. The ticket collector came to charge them their fare and included me in the price.

"Two adults and a child," said the ticket collector.

"He's not with us," protested the male traveler.

The ticket collector looked at me with an angry grin on his face. "Where is your ticket, *mocoso?*⁵" I didn't say anything; just shrugged my shoulders. The ticket collector went to the front of the bus and whispered to the bus driver.

*"Me lleva la...*⁶" shouted the bus driver as he brought the bus to a stop on a lonely, one-lane road. I was interrogated by the driver, who was demanding to know who I was with, where I lived, and where I was going. I answered honestly, and watched the driver rub his face with his hands as he processed each of my responses.

Few people had phones back then. However, the bus driver asked me what street my grandmother lived on, and somehow managed to call the grocery store on my grandmother's street. The bus continued on without the ticket collector or me. We waited on the road until another bus eventually came by and took us back to the old station. The ticket collector was then kind enough to drop me off at my grandmother's house.

---

5   *Bugger nose.*
6   *(Expletive: Motherf...)*

Grandmother Juana was angry, scolding me harshly. She was very upset that, rather than being an example for my brothers, I was causing the family shame. With contempt, she declared, "Your parents are in the United States working hard to be able to afford to send for you someday and this is how you behave?"

I didn't care. I didn't want to be apart from my family anymore. I shouted at Grandmother Juana and told her I would keep running away until I found my parents again. Frustrated and eventually fed up, my grandmother contacted my parents and told them about my adventures trying to find my way to them and, most importantly, her indignant intolerance.

I wanted my parents to realize they had no choice but to send for me as soon as possible. Eventually, I succeeded. Shortly thereafter, my uncle Lalo, my mom's youngest brother, decided that he would go north with me.

The Long Journey Alone

My Uncle Lalo and I rode together on the bus to Ciudad Juarez, on the Mexico-Texas border. We spent a night together at a cheap motel. That night, I had a terrible dream that men dressed in green uniforms (*La Migra*) busted the door open with machine guns and killed my uncle and me while we slept. I woke up in a cold sweat to the pounding of someone's fist on the door.

An old woman with light brown hair and yellow teeth introduced herself, stretching out her veiny and dry hand.

"*Yo soy tu abuela, huerco,*"[7] she said, winking at me. I looked up at my uncle who was asking me to go with her.

"We go our separate ways now, " he said. "You go with her, and I go on my own." My uncle was only twenty-one – young, unemotional, abrupt and determined to cross the border without me to hold him down.

I took my fake grandmother's hand and she led me as we walked through the unfamiliar streets of Ciudad Juarez. My heart beat against my chest with fear. I felt like a mouse exposed in an open field, waiting for the descent of the hawks. I wondered if my nightmare the night before was more of a premonition as I looked all around for signs of men dressed in green, holding machine guns. I wanted to disappear. I wanted to fade away forever and was quite relieved when we finally walked into a dark, long, dingy bar that reeked of warm beer and vomit.

Although it was early in the morning, several men were already sitting on the barstools smoking and drinking. The old lady picked me up and sat me on an empty bar stool, before she disappeared into the back of the bar behind tattered red curtains. She was gone and seemed not to be coming back.

I waited patiently, twisting back and forth on the bar stool while looking down at my shoes. My fear was mounting with each long minute she was gone. After what seemed an eternity of her absence, I rose from the barstool to go look for her when the

---

7   "*I am your grandmother, little piglet.*"

old man next to me reached over and held down my arm so that I would not be able to stand up.

"Don't worry," said the old man, trying his best to look serious and concerned. "You are safe here with me." Before long, he looked around and suddenly said to me, "It's time for us to go now. I am going to take you north to see your parents." He extended his big dry hand and I held it as we walked out into the vast, unknown streets. Every step I took away from the bar felt more and more frightening until every cell in my body was telling me that I was moving in the wrong direction. I was terrified!

We were not more than a block away, when I heard someone screaming behind us. It was my fake grandmother running toward us. She looked frightened and angry at the same time.

"*Que te estas creyendo Viejo borracho,*"[8] shouted my fake grandmother. She pulled me towards her and scolded me, telling me not to talk to anyone but her, and to keep away from everyone else. I realized, then and there, that I was almost kidnapped by an old, drunk man and that my life had been saved by this questionable character I knew as my fake grandmother. I felt like hugging her and thanking her. At the same time, I felt such fear in realizing that the old man planned to take me with him and I would have disappeared, possibly forever. I could have been attacked and left for dead, I thought to myself. I kept thinking about my mother and the pain she would feel hearing of my demise.

---

8   *"What do you think you're doing, you drunkard?"*

My fake grandmother took me to her small apartment and we waited until sundown. The entire time I was in her home, we rehearsed what I had to say in the event we were stopped by immigration officers while crossing the border. My fake grandmother was teaching me answers to the questions I might be asked. "What's your name? Where are you going? Who is this woman with you?"

Then, it was time to cross. My pretend grandmother told me I was lucky to be crossing with her and not having to go into the water like my other 'wetback' friends. She showed me to the back of her car. I climbed inside as she covered me completely with a blanket so that only my hair showed.

"Just pretend that you are asleep and don't make a sound. Don't speak. If anyone talks to you, respond only in the English I taught you. Tell them you are tired and that I am your grandmother," she instructed.

The car rode on top of a metal bridge until it rolled slowly to a stop. I could hear a man's voice talking to my fake grandmother in English. Although I was under the blanket, I could see the light of a flashlight shining into the car. A few more words were exchanged in low voices. Then...all was silent.

The car began to move again, at first very slow, then faster. I was nine years old and had the sudden realization that I had just crossed into the United States and was closer to my parents. I could think of nothing else but that I would see them again very soon. We drove for about an hour and came to rest on an old dirt road.

Soon, a car pulled up next to us. A nice looking woman looked into the car and greeted me by name, saying that my mother was her godmother at her wedding. *Someone who knew my parents!*

The car was packed with people and I was asked to climb inside. My fake grandmother waved me to them. "They will take you to your mother and father," she said very casually. I went to hug her, but she was gone. I peeked my head into the backseat of the car and found no place to sit. My mom's godmother saw there was no place for me and she waved me over to her.

"Come, you can ride on my lap," she graciously offered.

I climbed into the car and counted seven adults in that midsize car. Three sat in the front seat and four in the back, including Dona Castellanos, the godmother on whose strong and generous lap I sat for the entire car ride from the border to Aurora, Illinois, a suburb of Chicago where my parents lived. We drove nearly non-stop for more than twenty-four hours, stopping only to refuel in the most remote, lonely gas stations along the way.

The car ride was strangely silent. I am certain that my fellow travelers in that crowded car, mostly men, were thinking about the families, wives and children they were leaving behind in Mexico to risk their lives in a new, unknown land. Occasionally my Uncle Sam, our driver, would shout announcements. "We will be stopping in about three hours," I recall him saying.

"I will be the only person allowed to get out of the car. You can use the bathroom only where I say it is safe to do so. Do not use the bathroom anywhere we stop for gas or food."

Like an alarm going off in my head, I instantly felt an urge to go pee. At first, I held my tongue, afraid of getting yelled at by Uncle Sam. But I began to feel chills running up and down my arms and knew I had to speak. "I need to go to the bathroom now," I said, barely loud enough for Uncle Sam to hear.

"*Me lleva la....!*[9] Well kid, right now it is not possible. You're just going to have to hold it for a while; three hours or so," he responded in Spanish.

"No way!" I thought to myself, as I began to panic. I shifted uncomfortably on Dona Castellanos' lap.

Sensing my urgency, Mrs. Castellanos gently placed her hand on my back and said to me, "It's alright, my son. Do what you have to do."

I held my urge as long as I could, until I was unable to tolerate the pressure in my bladder and the extreme chills that multiplied all over my body. The first few drops of urine were quickly absorbed by my pants. But I could not stop the subsequent stream that came flooding out, spilling down my legs an onto the lap of Dona Castellanos. I sat as still as I could, bowing my head and looking down in shame at the urine that snuck out of the bottom of the leg of my pants and formed a small puddle between my feet. I felt small and very vulnerable.

---

9   *(Expletive: Motherf...)*

Dona Castellanos simply said, "It's alright, my son. Nothing to be ashamed about."

As we drove farther north and into Illinois, the December weather became unbearable. I had never felt such cold. Even though the heater was cranked as high as possible, a cold draft came through the old car, biting hard until my toes were numb.

Uncle Sam announced that we would be arriving late at night on Christmas Eve. He became more talkative, as if preparing us for the shock of entering the new and mythical world of *El Norte*, the place where all dreams come true, the land of milk and honey where money is swept up with a broom. My heart beat fast and hard against my chest as I imagined the faces of my mom and dad. Would they recognize me? Would I be able to recognize my little brothers, Luis and Pico? Uncle Sam's announcements became more frequent with every mile we drove and I knew we would be arriving soon.

"We will be in Aurora in four hours," he said. Then he announced three hours, then two, then, "We are just outside of Aurora." No sooner did Uncle Sam make that announcement than.....it began to snow! I had never seen snow in my life. My only experience had been eating shaved ice in paper cones filled with fruit toppings. It was magical. This truly was a new land.

Suddenly, without a final announcement or any fanfare, the car rolled into the dirt driveway of a giant, gray, two-story wooden house, unlike anything I had ever seen before.

One by one, we climbed out of the car, wobbling unsteadily, trying to recover the strength in our legs. I felt as though I was learning to walk all over again. The night air was cold and sweet with white snow falling in big flakes. Just as I was regaining some sense of control over my legs, a large woman with a kind face and black glasses came out to greet us. I had never seen her before, but I learned later that she was my Aunt Anna.

With every step I took, objects and people came in and out of focus as I kept looking for my mother. I was led through a large kitchen and did not see my mother. I was led through the living room, crowded with chairs, couches and other furniture, and did not see my mother. We turned into a hallway and I did not see my mother. The hallway opened up into a large, winding stair-case; still no mother. My frustration, exhaustion and fear welled up inside me. I followed the staircase part-way up as a deep, drawn out cry began to build in my stomach and throat before spilling out of me. I couldn't contain it anymore. Though I had been aided by helpful strangers, the loneliness of my journey and years of separation from my parents were finally unleashed in a torrent of tears and heavy sobs. I could not even see through the tears cascading out of me.

But amid my own wails, I heard something familiar. My cries were being echoed by those of my mother, who appeared at the top of the stairs, tearfully and joyfully shouting down to me.

"Hijo!" She cried. "Hijo, Hijo, Hijo!"[10]

---

10   *"Son! Son! Son!"*

She ran down the stairs towards me, and I sobbed as she wrapped me in her arms. I embraced her tightly against me. I was flooded by her familiar and comforting scent, the same one that I had desperately sought for two years when I pressed my nose to her letters.

We hugged and kissed each other. She did not yell at me for running away and I did not confront her for having left me behind.

At that moment, nothing could taint the love that I felt pouring out of my heart.

New Life in *El Norte*…Longing for Home

That was my first Christmas in the United States. While I was reunited with my mom, dad, and two youngest brothers, it was a very different Christmas than those festive *Posadas* I was used to, which celebrated the difficult journey of Mary and Joseph from Nazareth to Bethlehem, similar to the journey I had just taken. No one put their shoes outside their door for baby Jesus to fill with candy and toys. There were no gifts from the three kings and no festivities with neighbors dancing and children breaking *piñatas*. But we were together again and I showered my baby brothers with hugs and kisses. I was proud to be the big brother again and happy to be protecting them from every danger, real and imagined.

My family and I lived in one bedroom of a three-bedroom house that we rented from my grandfather. The other rooms, including the basement, were shared by some twelve other men who lived in the house, taking over every space and piece of furniture. They were all there to work and send money back to their families in Mexico. Though, not all the money made it back to Mexico.

Every weekend, starting with Fridays, there was an instant party as the men brought beer to celebrate their paychecks and the end of the week. Sometimes the parties lasted until early in the morning. And, more than a few times, the parties ended in fights and menacing threats.

But the fights and intolerance wouldn't just be for men in this new world. We kids would have to learn to endure, adapt, and occasionally fight, too.

The memory of my first day at school is as fresh today as it was then. I walked the eight blocks from our house to Lincoln Elementary School, as I tried to catch snowflakes on my tongue. I walked into the schoolyard excited to make new friends. I looked around eagerly, trying to connect with the various kids I saw, but no one greeted me or even came near me. Everyone looked so different than I did. They laughed together and spoke in English. Their blond hair and dull clothing made them all look so similar. I realized how much I missed my school friends back home.

Here we did not get together and march around the school before starting our day, nor did anyone place us in line to walk into the school in an orderly fashion. Instead, in America kids gathered outside, talking and playing in small groups. I was alone, watching and wondering what made me so different from the rest of the kids.

Although I had already graduated from the third grade, I had to repeat it in Illinois, because I did not speak English. I was the only Mexican in my school. Along with my Puerto Rican friend, Josie, and my Texan friend, Roy, we were the only Latinos.

My teacher did not speak any Spanish, nor was she amused by my lack of ability to communicate. She placed a desk for me in the back of the room, facing the wall, while she taught her class and I watched filmstrips with headphones on my head. Until then, the only person I had ever seen wearing headphones was the famous Mexican national news anchor, Jacobo Sabludovsky. I had watched the news every night, imagining that some voice in those headphones was telling Mr. Sabludovsky what to say, and he was simply repeating what he heard.

Being a quick learner, although at times not very observant, I falsely concluded that I was expected to repeat what I heard from my headphones. The children laughed at me, and my teacher began to lose whatever little patience she had. I was quickly labeled as "Mildly Mentally Retarded," and remained permanently in the back of the room while the class continued without me.

Over the early years, I began to have significant behavioral problems in school, which grew out of my constant fighting with other boys. I could not stand still for the racial slurs. "Wetback!" "Spick!" "Greaser!" These and other insults became my

34

nicknames. And, when I heard them, an invisible switch within me was turned on and I became a fighting machine. I would black out and would awaken while I was beating into a pulp whatever child dared to call me names.

I had already been suspended a few times when a boy named John and I got into the biggest fight that I can remember. The bucktoothed kid with a Polish-sounding last name kept spitting at me and telling me to go back to my country. He must have pushed me a little too far. I lunged for him, grabbing and punching him, much to my teacher's horror.

Mrs. Taylor frantically tried to separate us but couldn't. So, she hurriedly called Mr. Wildman, our Principal, who pulled at my legs while I clung to John's neck. After being pulled off the boy, I was promptly sent home.

A few hours later, two people from the school showed up at our crowded house. My mother was ashamed beyond belief that they were asking to speak to her. They told her that if I got into just one more fight, she would have to find some other place for me to go to school, because I would be *forever* expelled from Lincoln Elementary. Upon their departure, my mother cried with rage and shame.

Looking at me she said. "I am so ashamed right now that I can't even look at you! I don't understand you. Why are you behaving like this? Instead of being an example as the oldest, you are causing us great embarrassment. Why? Why?" She kept demanding to know why I was embarrassing her and being so irresponsible.

"I just want to go back to Guadalajara. I don't like it here. Let's just go back home and have it be like it was before. Remember when we all ate around the table and you gave us breakfast before we went to school, and when we got back you were there to greet us and hug us? Why can't it be like it was then," I shouted, feeling the pain and frustration of being an unwanted resident in a foreign land.

She scolded me, "This is not a vacation for us. We are not here to have a good time. We are here to work. We are here because we have to be. We have lots of debt that we have to pay off. We are here to stay and I need you to help out, not to make things more difficult." Her words poured over me like a bucket of cold water. I suddenly felt her shame and disappointment. I wanted my mother to be proud of me, but I had instead disappointed her and my entire family.

At that precise moment, I decided I would turn my life around and I would do everything within my power to make my mother and my family proud. From that day forward, my life would be about making them happy and proud of me, no matter what the price.

At 11 years old, I began to study day and night. During the summers, I worked pulling weeds out of soybean fields. I also started selling Christmas cards through a school program.

With the points I earned from my card sales I bought a
bright orange tape recorder, which I used to record the audio of
the popular television show, The Brady Bunch. I longed for my
family to be like that happy family. We had so much in common, I thought. They were also a family with six children, and,
perhaps, if we played along and did all we were supposed to do,
then we too could be just like the Brady Bunch. I recorded every
show and copied Greg's voice, practicing over and over, in an
attempt to erase my Mexican accent.

Before long, I began to get good grades and was listed on
the honor roll. I got involved in extra-curricular activities and
wore argyle sweaters and penny loafers. Further, and much to my
Grandmother Lidia's disappointment, I even became ashamed of
being who I was. (Grandmother Lidia was the grandmother who
had moved to the United States, years earlier, and who would
become a very powerful influence in my life, once again, as she
had been back in Mexico.)

Yet, no matter how hard I worked at fitting in and being
accepted, I still felt I was faking it and that I was not included as
an equal. That exclusion became most obvious when I joined the
Boy Scouts. With my own money, I proudly bought my uniform,
including handkerchief and patches. Still, when I would go to
the Scout meetings, I was always ignored by the leaders, and left
alone in the back of the room.

Nonetheless, I was determined. If education and hard work
were the keys out of poverty and into success, I would carve the

path for my entire family. I would achieve as much education as I could possibly achieve and gather as much success as possible, so that my mother and my family would never have a reason to be ashamed of me, ever again. From that one fateful, fight-filled day forward, my life became the incessant quest to make others happy with me, to never again be a burden to anyone, and to take on whatever responsibilities were necessary to make sure everyone liked me. Though I began to look successful and fit in on the outside, my spirit fell into a stony sleep... from which it would take decades to finally awaken.

So, What Are We Awakening To?

Our ancestors believed that life is like a dream, an illusion colored by the memories of our attachments. We become attached to experiences we don't completely understand. Intense joy and pain overwhelm our mind's ability to process the stimulation that is coming through and so these experiences scare us and cause us to want to hold on to the experience. The mind wants to hold on because it NEEDS to understand. It NEEDS to process what it could not process when it was young and overwhelmed. The way that the mind processes information is by holding on to these extreme experiences in order to find some explanation for why the extreme situation took place at all.

In my life, I began to live an illusion. I had been so stricken by these powerful childhood experiences that I never wanted them to happen again. Living in fear that they might happen again, I created a false self. I didn't know I was doing this, but it's precisely what was happening. My mind was holding on to these frightful experiences that were my childhood. But because I could not make sense of them, I stuffed them away, ashamed, and built an entirely new life around my running from those fears.

The problem is that sometimes there is just no clear explanation. Why me? Why did I have to go through that sexual abuse? Why did I have to have a father who was an alcoholic? Why did I have to come to a foreign country and be treated as a criminal all my life?

Well, the existential answer to these questions must be..... why not you? If we demand to know a rational explanation, or justification, for what transpired in our lives, then we hold on to the past in a self-obsessed insistence that demands an explanation from God, from the Universe, for something that may not be able to be understood. We hold on as a means of controlling what we feel we cannot   control. But control can give us a false sense of security. The ego feels justified, empowered, indignant, angry, separated and REAL! We like feeling REAL!

I sure felt real and alive as I voraciously pursued success for the following decades. But it was an aliveness born of fear, born of the desire to control my external environment. My past had created such terror that all of my faculties came to life to control every variable possible and make myself likable to everyone. I sacrificed my true spirit so that I might feel some sense of control and security.

Some of us come from thousands of years of self-sacrifice, where the beating heart itself was offered to appease the gods. Yet, our concept of God has evolved and now we recognize not only that the Creator does not need our sacrifice, but does not want it. It is not necessary to sacrifice any further. It is time, rather, to collect the interest on those thousands of years and millions of lives that did sacrifice for you to just HAVE or just BE who you really and fully are. The true security of life comes not from controlling our external environment by getting the best car, the best house, and a steady stream of money. Instead, true security and peace come from living the truth written on our hearts.

We come to fear the currents of the river of life. The river flows, forever changing, and these constant changes are scary. We fear that yet another sacrifice might be required and we fear we just may not have it in us. So we cling to what is safe, rather than embrace the newness of change and growth.

Our inner awareness tells us that this moment is eternal and that our consciousness continues forever, yet we still fear death because we don't fully trust in our true identity as sparks of creation. We like to feel in control because we are afraid of not being. We hold on to painful memories and experiences because we resist the lesson buried in the midst of our suffering. We don't just hold on to the overwhelming pain, often we hold on to pleasurable events that we want to experience once more – the rush we felt that first time at that party, the vacation, the intense sexual experience and other thrills which define our peak moments, but which become our dependence when they inevitably feel incomplete. We chase after the pleasure to escape the pain. Yet, most often, we insist on holding on to the fear and pain because we believe somehow the suffering makes our lives more real.

Holding on creates a script or a map we follow in life. We come to believe that life is really the script we adopted. We act out our drama and we defend this drama with every bit of our strength, because we believe that it is the only reality possible for us. We want to increase our joy and so we believe this must mean we have to forever outdo our last, greatest pleasure, forever striving for new highs. We want to avoid our pain and in the process we inadvertently give our hurts more power by attempting to block our memories of the past sufferings. We become obsessive about the pain we endured as a means of justifying our perceived limitations.

We look to increase our joy as if it were a quantifiable and tangible product. The reality is that our joy will be increased only when we come to realize that there is nothing to chase after, nothing to fight, nothing to resist, attack or defend against. The extended mind recognizes itself as the force that creates and that has always created. Thus, joy, peace, and bliss are not commodities to pursue. We do not find lasting joy and peace by possessing a particular toy, a bigger house or newer car, or by achieving some new level of career success. Rather, true and lasting peace and joy arrive through the process of surrender of ego and will to intuition, and the discovery of peace that comes from letting go of the need to control and force life. They are strictly internal processes. No external event or possession can bring lasting joy. Thus, the Awakened Mind comes to understand that it has the same power to create fulfillment and happiness as the Universal Mind. The Awakened Mind realizes that it is one and the same as the Universal Mind.

There is great power in the awakened realization, "I have created my life. I have attracted the people and circumstances that I needed in order to teach me what I needed to learn." All of this AWAKENING takes place in its right and proper time. If I realize that I created my life as it is, then I also realize I have the power to change it. So, we have an infinite number of choices in life, which includes the possibility of continuing to live our lives as defined by the pain that we have endured, or to make a radical transformation and affirm the generous, loving, creative force that has brought us to the grace of this present moment.

"Seamos humildes ante nuestro creador que
en esa humildad nos eleva a su hogar."[11]

…Grandmother Lidia

---

[11] *"Be humble before our Creator; for in that humility we are*
elevated to his home." Only by reuniting with our highest truth, rather
than all we have been told by society that we must be, will we ever walk
into the happiness and fulfillment we truly seek.

With this book you can go back to your past and recognize the power that carried you through. With a heightened, more generous perspective of your true identity, you will rewrite your present story. Your gifts and talents will begin to shine through. You will find that your gifts are just what is needed to best serve you in the present moment.

Think of your life as being a giant blank screen in a theater. This blank screen is capable of receiving an infinite number of movies. The movie you project comes from your mind and it is projected upon the screen that IS your life. Your life is simply the result of the thoughts you project. That is your reality.

So, if you don't like the movie being projected, you have the power to rewrite the script and project a new movie. You can change your life! Imagine the infinite possibilities opening before you! You define your reality based on the thoughts and beliefs you choose to retain. Let go, therefore, of those thoughts, feelings and behaviors that no longer serve you; they create a bad movie on that screen that is your life. When you let go of limiting beliefs you will begin to awaken to the endless possibilities, which are always at your disposal, and your life will become a wonderful adventure on that big screen.

You are awakening to your true potential and your true potential contains the ability to materialize whatever your mind is able to perceive long enough to see it manifest into reality. You are realizing that you are of the same nature and matter as the immeasurable, creative force that has brought everything in the universe into existence. And still, even beyond the imaginable universe, there lies the source of this invincible power. This force has guided gases and molecules of matter, vast darkness and unbearable light coming together and forming the physical world we inhabit. This is the force that has created everything and has been doing so since before the beginning of time. Our universe is the embodiment, the very evidence of that creative force in action.

Such a force also has an unimaginable intelligence, which propels it to expand and multiply itself in all directions. This force has also given you choice to direct creation by allowing you to define your reality. Is your life a celebration or a lamentation? You get to decide.

This is the eternal life giving force that is forever and ever growing beyond the limits of our imagination. This is who you really are. In its infinite wisdom, this creative force has chosen YOU in order to manifest itself and its will as your life.

Consciousness: The Individual and the Collective

Consciousness has an individual component as well as a collective one. The individual component of consciousness is called the ego. It is your sense of individuality and separation as well as the sum of your memories, perceptions, fears and attitudes. Your individual awareness can make you feel as though you are the most wretched person on earth AND also the most important.

Either way, extremes can make you feel unique or separated, until you feel as though you are the only person that matters.

Our egos are aware, but mostly only of their misperceived power and feelings of separation. According to our ancestors our sense of identity, what we call our 'ego,' is an illusion. You create your ego because you need to feel that things remain permanent and that you can control the ever-changing circumstances that surround you.

But life is an ebb and flow; a constant parade of changes and transitions. If we don't learn to flow with the tide, we can find ourselves struggling against great uncontrollable forces.

Our egos drive us to be competitive, insecure, afraid, retaliatory, angry, etc. All of these emotions express our feelings of separation and uniqueness. Some people love to emphasize how they are different from others in order to feel special. Some people believe that what makes them special is their race. Others believe their uniqueness rests in their economic power. Others use military violence to feel more powerful. Nonetheless, all of these people and ways of thinking are wrong.

People are special and powerful because they share the same spark of creation we all share. We have all been created by the same CREATOR. Someday we will all recognize that true power can be found only when we identify and operate within the spectrum of thoughts and behaviors which form the rhythm of the common force that has brought us all into existence.

Ego Is Separation

You can believe that good things happen to everyone else except you. You can have beliefs about yourself that are rooted in ego or separation. Just like the person who believes he/she is special and unique, the person who believes only bad things will happen to him/her is identifying from the same place of ego. The person entertaining such thoughts believes that a special set of rules applies to them and not to anyone else. "Nobody understands me" or "Nobody is better than me" are both statements rooted in separation. When you feel separated, you WILL eventually end up feeling unworthy and inferior. It's not your fault. Sometimes these thoughts of inferiority and separation were taught to you as a child. No doubt, you have been influenced by such teachings and, despite their damage to your life you have held on to them. At times, you even have identified entirely with these damaging thoughts.

> *"Si la educación te ensena avergonzarte de tu verdad,*
> *no aprenderás nada que le sirva a nadie."* 12

...Grandmother Lidia

---

12   "If your education teaches you to be ashamed of your truth, you will not learn anything that can serve anyone." You cannot bring life and joy to others, until you have the courage to live who you truly are.

Thus, you must become aware of your attachments and your fears. To do so, you must retrain your mind to focus on those thoughts that are true and productive and not on those falsely learned, devaluing lessons. You first have to become aware that you are attached to dysfunctional patterns and erroneous thoughts. You can become aware by practicing 'mindfulness,' or an awareness of the present moment as it unfolds. If you are able to see your emotions as transient and ever-changing, then you can learn to let them go. You don't have to feel that these changing storms define who you are. With detachment you can become liberated from your past mistakes and suffering.

Humanity is finally realizing that we are not all ego. We are much more than the prefabricated notion of identity we have purchased with our lives, the same prefab identities that are foisted onto us by a consumerist culture. When we brave up and drop the mask we wear in public, we will begin to learn how to look deeper into our true essence. This is the place from which we can tap into the infinite. From this place we will be able to access the great storehouse of *collective awareness.*

What is Collective Awareness, or Collective Consciousness?

The collective mind, or collective consciousness, contains every idea ever thought by every person that came before you. It is an inherited part of your experience and forms a bank of collected ideas and experiences which you inherit at birth. You are connected to this databank and can have access to this intuitive wisdom when you learn to quiet your mind in order to listen to your intuition, which is also known as your inner voice. You are always connected to this wealth of knowledge and can always access it for your benefit.

The collective awareness contains all of the thoughts, beliefs, dreams and aspirations of the ancestors from the beginning of time, right down to your individual life. You and I are critical components of this collective awareness. Every idea, every longing ever experienced is recorded somewhere in time and space. Such a vast store of treasure is available to you at any given moment. Imagine that! You can have access to the great mysteries of creation in order to help you find your intended path and bliss in life.

How Are Thought Patterns Formed?

For more than twenty five thousand years, our native ancestors have noticed that life is organized in cycles that include markers for days, weeks, months and eras. These cycles are also evident everywhere in nature. The earth and the moon revolve around the sun in predictable and measurable patterns. Winter gives way to spring and spring to summer. A seed becomes the potential that it already carries within. In the same manner, our thoughts are governed by the same rhythms and cycles than those evident in nature.

These predictable cycles of nature, time and thought, keep themselves constant unless they are interrupted by a new thought or new level of awareness. If you are unhappy, identifying and changing the disruptive patterns of your thoughts and behaviors will release the energy necessary for your transformation. A new 'thought' threatens the old pattern and creates disharmony with old patterns, disrupting the much-valued stability and homeostasis. At first, as the old paradigm begins to shift, there is resistance and discomfort. Such discomfort occurs until it forms chaos and imbalance. Slowly, always, out of the ashes of the old paradigm, a new one emerges. You begin to let go of an old way of doing things and at first, as you let go, your life may feel disorganized. Soon, you regain your balance and if you keep with your discipline, you will find that you have changed. You have transformed yourself into the person you always imagined you could be.

The more you go through life trying to resist change, the more your behaviors have a high probability of becoming too familiar and, as a result, rigid. When the pain caused by this rigidity becomes unbearable, you will begin a new cycle of awareness and so on. The new behavior is incorporated until it is once again familiar to you. The ongoing cycles of awareness must be fostered and must be received with loving kindness. Such cycles are necessary in order for us to continue growing. If we don't move with the ebb and flow of life, we stagnate, and stagnation is the equivalent of death.

How Can I Change Unhealthy Thought Patterns?

In this book, you will be guided through a process that will teach you how to eliminate negative thoughts and behaviors and replace them with thoughts more congruent with your true dreams and aspirations. Once you identify negative thoughts and behaviors, you can create a plan of action. Your plan of action is your map to guide your transformation. As you begin to implement this action plan you will begin to experience happiness and you WILL reconnect with your intended path.

This book is centered on the practice of using daily affirmations. These affirmations have been written to represent a central theme in the transformative process. You are expected to organize your schedule for seven days so that you are able to prioritize your commitment to live each day of the week guided by your affirmations and your plan of action.

Getting rid of your old thought patterns will require a bit of a sacrifice (and must continue beyond the reading of this book). You have to be willing to sacrifice comfort and familiarity in order to integrate new patterns. Your dependence on the familiar can be so addictive that you can prefer to keep negative or dysfunctional thoughts and behaviors simply because they are familiar. You can get used to a nagging relationship or almost any other ongoing discomfort because you are more afraid of changing your life than staying with the discomfort. But if you can push yourself to let go of these familiar ways of thinking, you will see more and more brilliant changes unfold in your life.

Your Potential, or *Tonalli*

In my first book, *The Promise of The Fifth Sun: Ancestral Journey of Self Discovery*, I talked about '*tonalli.*' Your *tonalli* is your unique energy, your soul, your calling, or your essence. The specific vibration of your individual embodiment which transmits and receives in a frequency all your own.

According to ancestral teachings, we all have a unique purpose that was set before the time of our birth. Your *tonalli* is this distinct voice inside, which tries to guide you towards your happiness and fulfillment. Your unique gifts and talents are expressions of your *tonalli*. This fingerprint of originality guides your path to your happiness, success and bliss, that is, if you have the courage to heed its directives.

The energy of your *tonalli* is unbound and contains an imprint of your true potential. Just as an acorn has a *tonalli* to be a mighty oak, your *tonalli* contains everything you need to live your most abundant life – i.e. your true potential.

Your true potential resides within the very core of your being. It has always been there, awaiting your discovery. That potential is never harmed or diminished, no matter how much pain and difficulty you have endured in the past. When you were born, your *tonalli* was perfect and complete. It contained all you needed to secure your success and to live a life of joy and peace. That potential remains within you, forever intact and unharmed. No matter what has transpired in your life, or how much time has passed, you can always reconnect to your *tonalli*. To reconnect, you have to re-learn the art of intuitive knowing, otherwise known as listening to your 'gut.' This is the wisdom that comes when you pay attention to that inner voice which forever seeks to guide you. Practicing mindfulness can give you a vehicle to reconnect to that inner knowing and purpose.

Can You Really Transform Your Life in One Week?

Yes, it is possible. In one week, you can BEGIN to develop the healthy habits required for deep and long-lasting change in your life. Everything is NOT going to change overnight or in one week. However, no matter how stressful or difficult your life has been up to now, you don't have to continue on a hindered path that leaves you feeling uninspired, anxious, depressed, over-whelmed and unfulfilled. Once you learn to tap into the creative powers of your mind and unlock your infinite potential, the path will be made clear and will open before you without obstacles. The power to transform your life lies within your ability to soundly choose those thoughts and to implement those actions that can bring you joy, peace, and happiness. In one week, you can crack open the shell that has been your life of illusion, and begin to see the patterns and negative beliefs that block your happiness. You can also begin to implement NEW behavior patterns and ways of thinking.

In recent years, a vast amount of research has focused on the power of our thoughts. By now, sayings like, *"Transform your thinking, transform your life,"* may sound like a clichés. Yet, in

essence, the secret is as simple as that…and also as difficult
as that. You see, much of our thinking is automatic, that is,
our mind is usually operating on a subconscious level. In other
words, we are not aware of the idle chatter we entertain and the
terrible things we say to ourselves. We are not fully aware of just
how our negative thoughts make us feel helpless and defeated.
Imagine the life of a person whose entire thought process
consists of the pain and injury they suffered in the past. Because
thoughts are powerful, people who hold on to their past suffering
manifest more suffering in their lives. It's a simple formula of
attraction. Positive attracts positive and negative attracts negative.
Thoughts and behaviors attract more of the same.

I understand that it may be difficult or even absurd to believe
that true life-transformation can occur in a mere seven days.
Yet in just seven days, this book will help you achieve two
critical goals:

1. **Identify the thoughts and behaviors that are keeping
   you from your happiness;**

2. **Show you how you can create a plan of action to
   bring about the life you desire.**

Like many people, you may have made several, if not many,
past attempts to make changes in your life, but something always
seems to pull you back to your old ways. When you regress to
the past, you are likely to feel defeated and convinced that the
life you want to live is more of an illusion than a reality.

Maybe life up to this point has brought you great pain, disappointment and disillusionment, and you feel reduced and defeated. Maybe you have wondered about the significance of so much suffering? While these feelings may be valid representations of your past experiences, such negative thoughts and feelings do not have to take over your life and do not have to define your reality, going forward. Nothing negative or painful that has ever happened in your past has power to determine your life. The only person with the power to align your life with its true purpose and intention is you. Only you can decide to step back in line with what is truly possible for you. That's right, *step back in line.*

Returning to Center

Pain, sadness and fear are normal and even healthy experiences every now and then. They can show us what is not our path anymore or can warn us of danger. However, when these emotions become our usual and customary reaction, pain and sadness stop serving their purpose and become calloused and rigid, blocking our vision and keeping us from being able to think and behave as we really are, deep down.

When this happens, we start to act out of our fear and our wounds. When we constantly give way to these emotions, our life becomes a persistent experience of unhappiness, sadness, anger, disappointment...and the list could go on forever.

If suffering is keeping you from being happy, the pain and fear you are retaining and experiencing should serve as a warning to indicate that you are off your intended path. If you are off, you can always choose to step back in line and re-align yourself with your true, intended path. Are you ready to let go of limitations and pain? Are you ready to do the work required? Are you ready to live your true path?

The fact that your past efforts did not produce the outcome you desired does not mean you are incapable of manifesting a fulfilling life. The power of transformation always operates under predictable and consistent universal laws. If you employ these laws accordingly, they will always deliver the results you seek. The universal power of transformation is functioning as adequately today as it always has. This power stands by and is awaiting your participation.

The laws of the universe are impersonal and they work the same for everyone. There is no person that is a worthless sinner, just as there is no person that is more deserving than others. You are not alone and are not subject to a separate standard then the rest of the world. You can access the power of creation and transformation directly. You don't need a mediator. If your desires are expressed clearly and unequivocally, then their demonstration can manifest instantaneously. If your hearts' desire is not manifesting, it is likely that you are still retaining and entertaining some fear, doubt or contradiction.

Sometimes we say we want to be happy, then secretly doubt whether we are worthy or we allow our fears and insecurities to keep us down. You can say that you are feeling miserable in your bad relationship. You can cry every day and at the same time you can be afraid of having to take the necessary steps in order to be free. You are afraid that the change you need may be financially, emotionally or logistically impossible and so you stay miserable but you complain louder. What you may not realize is that you have become dependent on things being just as they are. Perhaps, you need your spouse/partner to act in the manner in which they have been acting all along. This is necessary so that you can continue to blame him/her for your unhappiness.

When you decide it's time to change, nothing and no one will be able to stop you.

2

CHARTING THE COURSE

"Más vale prevenir que lamenter." [13]

...Grandmother Lidia

Evidence of the survival of ancestral teachings and examples of core principles have made their way into our modern awareness as 'new age' and other 'secrets' of health and wellness. Yet, these teachings are neither a secret nor are they really a new way of thinking.

Indeed our native Nican-Tlaca ancestors, the tribes of the Americas that include the Toltec and Aztec traditions, predicted this time of great transition and change. They stated that 'the children of light' would come to forget about their power and potential and instead fall asleep in a cloud of fear and hatred. Such slumber would end upon the rising of a new light, the new SUN of illumination. We have entered into the final era of Awakening, where we finally realize that we are creative beings

---

13 *"It is better to prevent than to lament."*

able to direct the force of manifestation with the power of our thoughts. We are so much more than physical beings impacted by the material environment that surrounds us. This is the end of the fifth and final sun, but not in the tragic apocalyptic sense, rather it is the end of a long cycle of limiting beliefs, where humanity came to falsely depend on the physical reality as an ultimate. As an example of this AWAKENING, we are realizing that matter is not as solid as we previously believed. Quantum physics teaches us that, at a subatomic level, matter responds to the thoughts and perceptions of the observer.

The kingdom of *Tonatiuh*, the Sun God, is at hand, as we begin to awaken to our true, divine and eternal nature. As we recognize that we are conscious, self-observant and reflective beings with strong powers of awareness, we discover the ability to create and recreate our own realities. The time of confusion is fast coming to an end as we prepare to enter into the new era of enlightenment.

History comes alive through our individual lives and we recognize that the oppressor and the oppressed reside within each one of us. Light and dark , good and bad, male and female; these opposing forces seek expression within us in some combination, or manifestation, that is somehow unique to each individual.

Your quirks, gifts and talents have been lovingly orchestrated by the Universal Mind in order to manifest in this specific place and time. You are the key to the sacred door; the essential ingredient in the soup of creation. Our ancestors predicted that this time in history would be marked by rapid changes and great confusion and loss. As evidence of this rapid transformation, we can look toward our politics, economy , environment and world events. Radical transformation has begun and how you choose to react will determine the fate of our existence. This level of transformation can be disorganizing and often frightening. Such is always the case whenever a person or a people evolve beyond previous limitations.

Yet, we must always remember that there is nothing to fear. Fear is a reaction of the ego and the ego is an illusion that we invented as an attempt to maintain a false sense of control over our lives and over forces that are beyond our control. We trust that there is a Universal Law that lovingly orchestrates all matter and events in order to bring the lessons of greater love we need to learn for our own transformation. The exact people, events and places you need will appear in the exact time you need them in order to teach you the lesson that is required for your evolution. We must be AWAKENED to these clues as they appear and to appreciate their meaning without becoming defensive or reactive.

When such messages reveal themselves in our lives, we typically try to find someone else to blame rather than accept the message needed for our own transformation. The rapid changes we are witnessing represent the end of a time cycle and the beginning of a new era. This is the time when oppressive systems fall apart and we are liberated, able to see with new eyes and feel with a new heart. We are finally able to obtain the Awakening we have been expecting for more than five hundred years. The ultimate wave of enlightenment, where fear and confusion melt, where the material realm must bend to obey the higher laws of energy and spirit, has already begun.

We no longer need to be controlled by our feelings of lack and limitation. We have an opportunity to realize the connection that we have to the earth, the infinite universe and to every other living being that we encounter. We can reclaim the ancestral wisdom and restore our individual and collective harmony and balance. We can learn to detach from our personal experiences and emotions long enough to study them and learn about the places where we get stuck. With certain detachment and curiosity, we don't have to be pulled into our pain and thus, we can begin to appreciate how the universe orchestrates every finite detail in order to teach and invite us to participate in the creation of our intended, unlimited life. The clues and directives we get from our intuitive voice are straightforward. We can take advantage of such clues, if we maintain a clear mind and an open heart to receive these messages. The process of AWAKENING begins to occur when we learn to identify the emotions and fears that have limited us in the past and we trade these for the undeniable power that comes from embracing our unity with the very force of creation.

These transformative messages are everywhere. As you become open to their existence, you will develop an ever-increasing ability to perceive them. These messages make their way into our lives in the form of coincidences or unusual events and situations. Across cultures and generations, central teachings continue to emphasize the connection shared between an individual person and the universal, collective Spirit, or Creator. Non-religious people might prefer to use concepts such as the collective consciousness or the universal force of creation, when referring to that mystery in back of all things, rather than to talk about God or a Creator. No matter what concepts are used to express the cosmic mystery, human existence has represented the embodiment of a creative force that becomes more complex the more 'intelligent' we become. We are awakening to the awesome realization that we are active co-creators of our lives and that we share, indeed we are of the same nature and content as the Universal Mind.

Today, research in consciousness studies and advances in quantum physics reinforce these ancient teachings. We understand that our thoughts are so powerful that they have the ability to impact the world around us. Our thoughts are projected outward and impact matter at the sub atomic level. We've come to know that something becomes real only after we focus our thoughts on the object or situation we are observing. Your observation and your thoughts and feelings about what you are observing create your reality. You judge and determine what you observe as being either positive or negative.

People who have experienced joy and harmony; who have been nurtured and loved as children are more likely to see life as a great and giving adventure. People who have suffered greatly and have experienced repeated exposure to pain and trauma can perceive life as difficult, painful, limiting, frightening, and depressing. The more pain we experience, the more likely we are to protect ourselves from further perceived pain until we become rigid and mistrustful and all we are able to recognize is restricted by our experience of suffering. Suddenly, our lives can feel as though we are living a bad dream that never ends.

We begin to doubt that good things can ever happen to us. We have trouble trusting people and the pain of the past seems to find constant expression in our present lives.

Suffering in life may be a reality, but it is not the final verdict or a necessary requirement. We suffer when we attach ourselves to some memory or to a sense of how things ought to be. We tell ourselves we need to understand why certain painful experiences happened to us or we need to be in control of the ebb and flow of life. While we can all become attached and fixated, we all can also learn to let go. Although we might have learned that sacrifice, pain and suffering make us stronger, these false teachings can also block us from living an abundant and joyful life. If your life seems like a dream that is limiting and painful, you can wake up and alter the dream.

You can reclaim all of the power and truth of the divine reality. You can AWAKEN to a life of infinite possibility and tap into the creative force which is always seeking to interact with you and to make you aware of the multiple and simultaneous realities available to you at any given time. The intuitive wisdom and knowing at the center of your being has never been harmed or diminished. Although in tough times, you may feel discouraged and alone, know that you can always learn to reclaim this infinite source of power. You can alter your thinking and plant the seeds that will bring forth a new, peaceful and joyous life. Yes, in just one week you CAN AWAKEN to your true potential!

The Power of Changing Your Thoughts

"Los pensamientos son una fuente poderosa de energia. Los pensamientos tienen la habilidad de crear el mundo material en el que vivimos." [14]

...Dr. Jorge Partida

Because thoughts and the words that grow out of them are so powerful, it is absolutely imperative to identify and change them as part of the process of AWAKENING, which this book will help you to accomplish in your life. This is why the incorporation of Affirmations and Meditations (as well as Journaling) is so critical to this process. Using these tools you will both identify destructive thought patterns you carry with you (through Journaling) and learn to replace them with new thought patterns (through Affirmations and Meditations) that serve your highest good and lead you to greater happiness.

---

14 *"Thoughts are a powerful source of energy. Thoughts have the ability to create the material world in which we live."*

Our lack of happiness is simply our conscious or subconscious tendency to automatically and repeatedly react to what appears to be true. We base our experience of reality on a collection of painful past experiences that we carry with us wherever we go. We hold on to thoughts that are erroneous or misguided. Your thoughts go before you. In other words, whatever you believe eventually becomes your reality. The reality you are currently living, the physical environment, the relationships, circumstances and situations in which you currently find yourself, are the logical outcome of thoughts you entertained sometime in the past. Oftentimes, your greatest fears manifest in your life because you spent so much time obsessing over them.

You live your reality based on the sum total of the thoughts that you retain. You use the reactions you receive from others to reinforce your beliefs about life. If you are unhappy with your present life, rather than finding others to blame, take a look at the thoughts and beliefs you are entertaining and retaining.

By changing your erroneous thoughts and subsequent behaviors, you can change your life. This cannot be overstated. Most people simply do not realize how incredibly powerful our thoughts are. And, if you learn to change your thoughts you can change your life. By changing your life, you can change the world!

As mentioned in Chapter 1, in order to AWAKEN, you must be willing to let go of the false comfort and familiarity provided by your dependence on habitual patterns. It might seem difficult at first to try to change old patterns. Although you might become aware that you have developed patterns of behavior that no longer serve you, not getting caught in the trap of endless repetition, takes commitment and constant awareness or 'mindfulness.' Not getting caught in the trap also requires a willingness to experiment with the new and unfamiliar world, which is located outside of the comfort of your old familiar habits.

Developing insight and awareness is a critical step, but having insight often is not enough. You also need a willingness to entertain new thoughts and try on new behaviors. These new thoughts and behaviors at first may seem strange and foreign, but that is precisely the point. You have to be willing to experience discomfort and the unfamiliar in order to break out of habitual thoughts and behaviors. In other words, you cannot be a new person and still think and behave the same old way. Are you ready? If so, then consider this...

Continuing Limiting Life Patterns, Actions, and Thoughts

A child that throws a temper tantrum learned to do so because the temper tantrum once got him what he wanted. If you continue to throw temper tantrums as an adult, you will most probably not get your way. Temper tantrums rarely work for adults, but that doesn't stop us from trying to make them work.

We attempt to force our agenda by threats or coercion and often, because we are so used to our automatic behavior, we may not even be aware of our actions. You cannot eliminate these patterns if you don't know you are practicing them. You will be able to get rid of your limiting thoughts and behaviors when you recognize that these do not produce the same rewards you used to get. Now, when you insist on getting your way every time you interact with someone you love, rather than those old patterns working, you find that the person you love begins to create distance from you. If the reward is not available, the behavior that sought the reward will also disappear (this is called 'extinction'). It may not be immediately obvious to you just how your unhealthy behaviors are rewarded. But rest assured, if you are maintaining an unhealthy behavior it is because you are experiencing some indirect payoff which is also called a secondary gain. What are the secondary gains that are presently holding you back?

"El que rico se hace por lo que roba y lo que toma pagara muy caro el abuso de confianza que el Creador le ofreció." [15]

…Grandmother Lidia

We all develop harmful habits. For example, yelling at your kids might make you feel like you've let off some steam. This momentary relief and release would be the indirect payoff. Yet the reward doesn't really work in the long run because the stress, guilt and tension you feel afterwards have disrupted the harmony of your home and your internal sense of balance.

---

15   *"He who becomes rich by what he steals and what he takes will pay very dearly for the abuse of the trust that the Creator gifted him."*

The Pull to Regress

Humans are creatures of habit. We like to feel we have mastery and control over our environment. Our habits and fixed patterns organize our lives and give us a sense of control. This is why changing patterns of thoughts and behaviors that took years to develop is no easy task. When we make an effort to break long-standing patters, we are likely to feel awkward. The unfamiliarity and stress with what is new can represent a strong pull to want to return to the old, familiar way of doing things. Beware of people and circumstances that try to pull you back. When you begin to change, you also show others a mirror of themselves. When you change, everyone else around you also has to change how they relate to you. But most people want the security of their lives staying the same, which includes you staying the same and acting the way you always have.

Additionally, there is a tendency for humans to regress to a previous level of functioning when under stress. This tendency to regress under stress can make you feel that you are moving backwards rather than forward. "I thought I was already past this point? Why am I still making the same mistakes after all this time," can be discouraging thoughts during the process of transformation. A drug addict can feel as though he/she constantly has relapses that make recovery seem impossible, but with each subsequent relapse, there is always something significant that has changed forever. We are just not trained to look for the subtle differences and can mistakenly believe that we are not evolving. When you commit to your transformation, you must be willing to fight through the initial stage of discomfort. Resist the temptation to regress until the new thought and behavior become familiar. Don't punish yourself or allow yourself to wallow in self-pity. This tendency to feel self-punitive can be a good excuse to regress and to abandon your progress. Reward yourself for the changes you have made, even when these changes seem small and insignificant. Give thanks for the people and circumstances in your life which support your further evolution and soon you will see that the process of Awakening is easy and self-revealing.

On Changing Patterns

There are seven steps involved in changing old, unhealthy patterns into new, joy-producing ones. Below, you will find a brief description of each step. This book devotes one chapter to each of the steps. It will be helpful for you to learn to recognize how and when you move from one step to the next, not just for each of the next seven days. These seven steps will be of great use to you as you further pursue this process, far beyond the point where you have finished the book.

But don't worry so much about having to memorize or do heavy mental work. The Affirmations you are asked to use each day of the week correspond to each of the steps below. That's right. The Affirmations are written to perform their steps. You will be performing the steps simply by engaging in the Affirmations, Meditations and Journaling Exercises prescribed in each chapter. You will be encouraged to perform these exercises twice each day.

The Seven Steps

1. **Awareness:** An ability to recognize discomfort or unease and to begin to localize the nature and extent of such discomfort. The ability to recognize that something is out of balance.

2. **Identification:** The ability to pinpoint the exact nature and source of identified discomfort.

3. **Interruption:** The ability to halt the typical trajectory of fixed patterns of thoughts and/or behaviors.

4. **Incorporation:** The ability to try on new behaviors and/or thoughts. Incorporation causes a disruption or imbalance in the previous patterns of thought and/or behavior.

5. **Release:** The ability to consciously let go of previously incorporated thoughts and behaviors that have now been identified to be unhealthy or limiting. This can be done through ritual and/or incorporation of new thoughts and behaviors.

6. **Assess:** The ability to measure progress and movement from a fixed, baseline to a pre-established point of evaluation (as an example, taking a pre-test at the start of a week and taking a post-test after completion of exercises at the end of the week).

7. **Reward:** The ability to recognize movement toward a desired target and to mark that progress with a statement or action that, in some fashion, reinforces the positive movement and gives an incentive to the person engaged in the art of transformation.

How to Apply the Principles of Transformation in Order to Change Your Unhealthy Patterns

Follow these steps, as laid out in the following chapters, and you will be able to break any thought or behavior that is limiting you. As you implement these steps, pay close attention to the resulting resistance that may occur as you begin to change. Remember that every thought or behavior pattern that you have adopted has been kept in motion because it once worked for you.

If you are 'resisting' it means you are afraid and may not want to let go of something or don't want something to happen the way it is happening. In other words, you are 'resisting' where life is leading you, and that resistance causes unhappiness or pain. Your resistance represent an attachment to a notion of how things ought to look or be, but remember that your perception is limited by your experiences. What awaits you is very likely far better than what your limited perception can imagine.

Resistance is created when we are convinced our wishes or desires are more important and powerful than the intentions of life, itself. For example, we often carry bitterness and resentments when someone hurt us in the past; perhaps when a lover or friend left us. Resistance, in this case, comes in the form of wanting reality to be different from what it is, such as wanting the person back or wanting the person to have been nicer to you. But resistance, wishing something were different, and the subsequent resentment that emerges, neither changes reality nor impacts the person who left you. Held resentments only make YOU miserable. No matter how angry you get, no matter how long you hang onto your version of 'the truth,' your fixated attachment has zero impact on others and on the events transpiring before you. So, you are carrying around bitterness *for no reason, at all*. And when we carry negative emotions, they only eat away at our insides; they only rob us of joy and the lightness of being. Resentment, bitterness, anger, and even sorrow are all forms of resistance that block the natural flow of life's joyful energy.

On Mindfulness

Mindfulness can also be called 'awakened awareness.' Practicing mindfulness will give you entry into the vast treasures of the collective mind. How? Try to think about this very precious moment you are in, right now. What are you lacking? What are you missing? What is possible for you? Do you see how this moment is perfect, without your intruding fears and worries, desires and passions? This moment is sheer infinity, perfection, and potential.

This means that you can have access to the infinite source of all awareness, the collective consciousness that represents the intelligence of your true self. The more mindful and aware you are, the more you are able to use the unbound power of creation and to use the magnificence of the universe to construct your ideal life. Mindfulness and the ability to remain centered enable you to feel the power of creation speaking from within you through the voice of your intuition.

It is vitally important that you learn to listen to your intuitive voice. There are countless people willing to tell you what to do. If you doubt your own power and true nature, you are likely to feel that the opinions of other people matter more than yours. When you believe that others matter more than you, you will likely forego your own intuitive knowing in favor of others' opinions. However, if you listen to your inner knowing, your intuition and inner voice will guide you to actions and thoughts that feel right for you.

Your inner voice is found at the center of your silence. This is why meditation, or quieting the mind, is such an important skill to learn. You have to learn to tune out all the noise from the demands of others, from the bombardment of information from the world and from your past in order to hear the voice within you. *Always trust this intuition and inner knowing because it will always lead you to your greatest joy.*

We can USE our thoughts to achieve a direction. That is, we can think for ourselves and move in the direction of our thoughts, but the direction itself is communicated by Creation or the Universal Mind through our intuition. This intuition expresses itself as a vision or a felt feeling, a gut reaction that speaks through silence. Learn to trust this quiet voice rather than relying on the voices of other people. Keep in mind that listening to others' opinions and desires for your life is exactly what led to your falling asleep in the first place. Reclaim the voice of your intuition and AWAKEN to your unlimited potential.

The same loving force that constructed everything in the universe waits for you to recognize that you are of the same source and substance. Once you recognize that you are one with that force, you will be able to speak your word with power and certitude, and you will be able to direct that power to construct the life you so desire. When you learn to recognize the perfection of the present moment just as it is, you will be able to focus your thoughts and direct the force of creation. You will understand the wisdom of the moment and the impact that each moment has in your life. You will experience a profound sense of power as you learn to reduce the noise and clutter that typically gets in the way of your optimal functioning.

Exercise: The Ecstasy of Doing Dishes

You don't have to engage in hugely deep or dangerous activities in order to practice mindfulness. In fact, it helps to be fully present even while performing every mundane detail of life. For example, you can practice mindfulness and become enlightened even while you are doing the dishes.

Try this: Go wash your dishes! Even if you are not the type of person to ever lift a plate, try to just wash a dirty plate. Become aware of the water running through your hands. Don't entertain worries or concerns while you do this. Just focus your thoughts and feel how the water and the soap caress your hands. How much joy can you surrender to as you realize that water comes out of the faucet automatically? How grateful can you allow yourself to feel as you count the thousands of bubbles that gather themselves between your hands? Your hands are obedient and respond to your mind's gentle command. You may even forget you are performing a chore as you feel the joy of life move through you at this moment. Your heart beats by itself and your breath is automatic. You are fully present and alive and you are not concerned about your problems, suffering or pain. You may even feel as though 'you' have disappeared and have suddenly been connected to all of creation.

The more you practice mindfulness, such as in this small exercise, the more you will learn to create ever-growing spaces of peace and tranquility in your life. The more these moments increase in your life, the greater joy and peace you will experience. Mindfulness is a discipline and like all others, it requires practice and commitment. The more you practice mindfulness, the easier it will become.

How to Use this Book

Each chapter of the book guides you through some core concepts that are often explained as a story to illustrate the concept. The concept is designed to work on multiple levels. If you prefer to know the theory behind actions, the story and concept will help you better understand the nature of what is going on, as well as the rationale. For those who prefer just the action steps, the Affirmation, Meditation, and Journaling Exercise sections will move you through the challenges and insights of your path to greater AWAKENING.

You don't have to do much to implement this week of change. The central practice for this week of transformation requires you to complete three simple steps:

1. Read the Daily Affirmations Every Morning and Night

Each day of the week is imbedded with a necessary step in this transformative process. As you read the affirmation and meditate on its meaning, you will actually be implementing one of the transformative steps, each day of the week. As you read the daily Affirmation, try to maintain your thoughts focused on the theme of the affirmation throughout the day.

Read the affirmation of the given day aloud. Think about the meaning of each word as you read it. Savor the words and let them hit your mind and heart. Take a few seconds of silence and then read the affirmation again. Two or three times a day, stop yourself and try to recall as much of the affirmation as you can. Check back and read the affirmation for accuracy.

How accurate was your memory?

What did you remember?

What did you forget?

What did you misunderstand?

2. Meditate on the Significance and Theme of the Affirmations Every Morning and Night

Don't let any responsibility or distraction keep you from reading your affirmation. You may choose to copy the affirmation on a piece of paper and carry it with you wherever you go. Pay attention to your feelings as you think about what you have just read. Do you feel energized and excited? Do you have doubts or fears? Write your thoughts down in your journal (see next section) and keep track of these thoughts and reactions throughout the week. It is not necessary to be alone or to do anything different during your week of transformation.

3. Journal Every Morning and Night After Your Affirmation and Meditation

You will need to keep a journal to write down some of your observations and thoughts throughout this week of transformation. A journal can be very helpful in revealing patterns and themes that may provide greater insight into your inner self.

You can select a nice journal you would like to keep to remember your week of transformation, but any regular note book will work just as well. You will need at least two blank pages to journal for, each day of the week. On the left side of your journal, keep track of events that transpired during your day. For example, at twelve o'clock you had an unexpected run in with an old friend you had not seen in years.

Even when you feel nothing out of the ordinary transpired in your day, try to keep track of events of the day and times when these occurred. On the right side of jour journal each day, write down the thoughts that come up for you as you read and meditate on each daily affirmation. Review your journal entries as you prepare to go to sleep:

- *Did you have an opportunity to read your affirmation more than once a day?*

- *What was happening when you were reading your affirmation?*

- *What changes in your thoughts and behavior can you begin to identify?*

To start your week of transformation, set up your schedule to make sure that you are able to begin each day of the week with at least fifteen minutes of quiet time. Allow yourself these minutes of silence to read your daily Affirmation and to meditate on its significance. Try to visualize how your day will unfold. Project yourself onto your day. See the people that you will encounter and imagine that all of your meetings and affairs will be successful.

Before you start your day of work or daily routine, allow yourself these fifteen minutes of silence and meditation. This is your time to be still and calm your mind. Pick up the book and read the Affirmation of the day aloud. Close your eyes and let the message of the affirmation sink into your mind. Take your time to complete your Meditation and after you spend this time in

silence, read the Affirmation aloud for a second time. As
you get ready to start your day of work, try to visualize yourself
having a positive and affirming day in which all of the experiences
and individuals you wish to attract will appear before you. Now
you are ready to embrace the day. When the day is done and
you are ready to wind down, set aside fifteen minutes in the
evening to jot down your thoughts and perceptions of the day
in your journal.

Read the Affirmation one last time before you journal and
think about the significance of its theme for your day of activity.
How does the theme apply to the events that transpired throughout the day? Go through the events of the day and journal your
thoughts and reactions, particularly as they relate to the theme
of the Affirmation you just read. Pay close attention to your
thoughts and reactions. What feelings and emotions come up for
you? Make sure that you document these in your journal. You are
setting out to change those thoughts and behaviors that do not
serve you and this work requires discipline and commitment.

Maintaining a daily account of your progress through your
journal is critical to highlight patterns and to show you material
hidden from your awareness. As stated before, your journal
should be organized with the left page dedicated to documenting
information about your day. The right page of the journal should
be reserved for your insights, thoughts and perceptions. Jot down
a brief description of the day's events and pay close attention to
describe your thoughts and feelings, regarding those events.

Be patient with yourself. This is a week of investigation and awareness. You are going to observe yourself as you would a stranger, without attachment, judgment or defense for your thoughts and actions.

Taking a little personal distance is important because your emotions and feelings are so closely interconnected to your actions and behaviors. And, again, by journaling and getting the thoughts and feelings outside of yourself you can look at them more clearly and learn to assess and change them. Further, the fact that you are able to ask life's profound questions and answer them in your journal is evidence that consciousness is at work, that you are becoming mindful, and that your life is changing even faster than you realize!

3

DAY 1: AWARENESS: ASSESSING YOUR LIFE

"Camarón que se duerme se lo lleva la corriente." [16]

...Grandmother Lidia

Destiny and fate play a critical role in ancestral teachings. Our ancient native fathers and mothers taught that each of us is born with unique talents and gifts and that our birth is timed just right so that the world can most benefit from our contributions. History is full of stories where heroes work hard to avert their fate and in the process run right into their destiny. Oedipus, perhaps the most famous example, learned of his fate to kill his

---

16   *"Shrimp that fall asleep are carried away by the current."* Meaning: If we don't remain aware and awakened, we can be taken away by the pull of the currents of life. Interestingly, *corriente in* Spanish also translates to *cheap, everyday* or *generic* – meaning popular thought or mindless acceptance of things as they are. Thus, the alternate understanding of corriente deepens the meaning of this ancient truism: *Those who do not live awake and live deliberately can be swept up and swept away by a cheap or generic life that lacks true meaning.*

father and marry his mother. In the process of running away from his predicted destiny, he tried running away from home. He later learned that he was adopted. Therefore, running away from what he thought was his home actually sent him to confront the destiny he was trying so hard to avoid.

Attempting to guide me to discover and follow my destiny, my Grandmother Lidia was always warning me about dangers and pitfalls that most often I simply could not see. Rather than think about her messages, I often dismissed her warnings and, at times, even seemed to do exactly the opposite of what she recommended perhaps as a means of proving her wrong and exercising what I thought was my superior individuality.

When I was a college student, I felt I knew it all and, I am embarrassed to say, sometimes thought of my grandmother as uneducated and old-fashioned. One of her constant warnings cautioned against the desire to have and accumulate:

" La persona que quiere algo puede facilmente ser controlada por la promesa de aquel que dice poder cumplirle ese deseo." [17]

…Grandmother Lidia

To someone like me, who had a hunger to achieve massive success, this warning seemed to be in direct contradiction to

---

17 *"The person who wants something can easily be controlled by another's promise of meeting that desire."*

my unbridled desire to conquer the world, to prove my special gifts and talents and to satisfy my insatiable hunger to have it all. Remember, I had 'fallen asleep' at a very young age. On the outside it looked like I was running toward success. But, in truth, on the inside, deep in my soul, I was running from my fears of letting people down, fears of not being liked, and fears of being a disappointment and a shame to those who knew me. I could not live my true destiny, which Grandmother Lidia was trying to help me discover, because I was so obsessed with my fears and running from them and letting them shape everything I did.

While fate and destiny play a critical role in our ancestral wisdom, we always have free will. Yet, the only true choice we ever have is whether we will say 'yes or 'no' to our intended path. Sometimes we say no to our fate out of ignorance, believing that something even greater waits for us outside the bounds of the straight and narrow path prescribed for us by the Universal Mind. Sometimes we say 'no' out of pride, perhaps because we want what we think is MORE (even though it never is, despite out-ward appearances), believing that we know better than our destiny.

Ultimately, we are all on a journey of self-discovery and when we say 'no' to our intended path, we only take a temporary detour, but in the process we always learn about life. When the lesson is obtained, we return to our intended path, having gained a greater understanding of ourselves and a deeper appreciation for the detours because we come to know them as the precious lessons that re-affirm the truth we tried to avoid.

At age 11, I had left my intended path. I succumbed to the notion that success would fulfill me and make people love me more. I had also given in to my fears of disappointing my mother and family. So, I did everything I could to run as fast and as far as I could in life. I let my fear drive my life and push me hard toward maximum success.

"No todo lo que deslumbra es oro." [18]

…Grandmother Lidia

But no matter how much success I earned, I was still leading a life that was driven by fear, not love and passion. It was an illusion. I had no sense of a 'calling,' or purpose in life, except to not look foolish, not fail, and not disappoint anyone – ever. I had fallen asleep in life, having completely given in to my greatest fears. No longer was I impelled by a love for the glorious creature God had made me to be, but was now driven by the fear of what people would think of me if I did not look right, talk right, and do all the right and successful things. I had lost my identity to the fear of looking foolish and the fear of failing. No longer did it matter who I truly was; all that mattered was what people thought of me. Trust and love had given way to fear. The real

---

18   *"Not everything that shines is gold."* Don't get carried away by appearances. Success, toys, possessions, and money may look wonderful, but they seldom bring the true happiness we seek.

little Jorge had been put to sleep – by ME – by the monumental fear of disappointing anyone ever again.

I learned that my true identity was a source of shame. When other kids taunted me for being different, when I thought that fitting in would buy me success, when I worked for the money and the title and not for my passion, when I allowed others to control me and judge me, I fell asleep. I fell asleep to my inner voice. I memorized accents and sound bites that came from the producers of fame and in the process I lost track of my own inner voice.

The process of Awakening has come when I have accepted that the detours I have taken have only brought me back to an inevitable truth and realization. You can run and you can hide, but you cannot escape the reality of your life. When we stop running and recognize that self-knowing and self-acceptance only lead to greater power and greater peace, we stop fearing and we start living.

I have finally learned to give myself permission to live my life guided by MY inner voice, even when it disappoints others around me. I have learned that, no matter how hard we work to please others, they may never be satisfied. You may give all you have and still not give what others want or need; and, as a result, you will never get the love, appreciation, approval, or attention you thought you were purchasing. When you live your life guided by your inner voice and you allow life to guide your path, you may disappoint those that have tried to control you, but you will discover that you are stronger and more powerful than you ever imagined.

Awareness

The first step in changing unhealthy thoughts and behavior patterns is simply to become aware of our feelings and reactions. We are not born able to speak about our emotions. On the contrary, when we were children and we showed emotion, we were often made to feel ashamed or weak. Emotional expression is a skill we have to learn.

Most of the time, we go through life largely unaware. While we are spending time with friends, our minds are usually wandering and thinking about our problems or other concerns. Our addiction to pain and fear has the effect, not only of blocking our happiness, but also of distorting our ability to strive beyond our comfort zone.

We have become accustomed to looking at life from the perspective of a disgruntled and unwilling participant. We come to view life from a critical perspective, always looking for the imperfections, to criticize and to emphasize what we don't have, what is wrong and what is missing in our lives. We compare our lives to those of the rich and famous – the seemingly fabulous people who appear to have it all without any concern in the world. We strive to live that same life, forgetting that such air-brushed fantasies are designed only to increase our hunger to consume. The more we consume, the more we want; the more we want, the emptier we feel.

The first step in changing our fixed patterns is to become aware that we even have them. We have to recognize that certain patterns have been reinforced to the point that they can be activated automatically. Sometimes, when we are driving down a familiar street, we forget to focus on where we are going. We don't know if we crossed a green light, but we assume we did because everything seems fine. It is as if we are driving on auto pilot.

Painful experiences and fears can be carried for years and can hide right in the very tissue of our muscles. Our bodies hold on to painful memories which are carried right in every cell in our body. We tend to react by holding on to these 'instantaneous' responses to perceived pain. Such constant tension causes us to become mentally fatigued and physically ill. Constant tension forces us to react impulsively and habitually.

How Pain Makes Us Rigid

Feeling pain DOES serve a purpose in our lives. Pain can protect us by teaching us about danger. Yet, experiencing pain over and over can lead us to believe that pain and fear are our central reality. Over time, we take ownership of these beliefs and we record them in the hard drive of our minds, to the point that we may not even be aware such beliefs still exist. In the meantime, we become alienated from the truth of who we truly are. Our lives become characterized by confusion, anguish and suspicion.

"Dios aprieta, pero no orca." [19]

…Grandmother Lidia

Think of a time when you have been hurt, intentionally or by accident. What did this experience teach you? What did you begin to believe about yourself and others as a result of this experience?

It would not be uncommon if you found yourself backing away from others by becoming cautious and guarded so that you wouldn't get hurt again. You may believe that this response serves as a way of protecting you against future pain. Yet, over time, such beliefs are not really protecting you or serving your needs as you might think; quite the opposite. The energy of your thought goes out like a radio wave. You send out a frequency that lets those around you know just how you are feeling. Soon, others begin to distance themselves from you or even treat you badly. Without being aware, you have created distance between yourself and others. You have an increasing desire to protect yourself while, at the same time, you are still feeling a strong and sincere desire for closeness and intimacy.

We create our suffering by magnifying all that is wrong in our lives. If we have endured great pain, we can spend much of our time and energy remembering our great suffering and

---

19 *"God squeezes, but he doesn't choke."* God applies pressures and difficulties to our lives NOT to break us, but to challenge us and move us to the greater good he has in mind for us to both live and become.

thinking about the persons that have harmed us. The more we think about how much we have suffered, the more suffering we attract, until we get to the point where our thoughts of suffering and pain block our ability to perceive any other reality.

Continued exposure to suffering and pain creates a tendency to view life from the experience of hurt. Because you are hurting, you can come to believe that you are not worthy of happiness, or that you are bad, less than others, incapable, ugly, fat, dumb... the list goes on and on. You can hold on to these false beliefs until they determine all you perceive. Soon, it is as if you are wearing dark glasses and you come to believe the whole world is wrapped up in this darkness. All that you are capable of seeing is visible through the lens of suffering, lack and limitation. But these lenses are not permanently fixed on our face. We can take them off. In the same manner, no amount of misinformation or false teachings can affect you forever. You have the power to change your thoughts and your experiences of suffering. You can unblock painful events and memories from your mind and release the energy needed to live a life of joy and satisfaction.

First, you have to determine how and where you got stuck. Remember that we get stuck when we hold on to either very painful or pleasurable experiences.

Below are the exercises for Day 1, which can help you determine hidden patterns of behavior that are likely blocking you from success and true happiness. In addition to helping you determine where you are stuck, today's exercises will assist you in beginning to become unstuck. Are you Awakening? Is your life changing in the direction of your soul's desire? The best person to judge whether you are changing or not has got to be yourself.

Day One

Task: Setting Your Baseline

1. AFFIRMATION

General Understanding of Affirmations

The moment that you catch yourself having identified a false teaching, replace that false teaching with an Affirmation. An Affirmation is a declaration of truth. As an example, you might catch yourself entertaining a false notion such as, "I am so dumb." Even though some deep part of you knows that this is not a true statement, there you are entertaining the thought and allowing yourself to be carried away by it. As you catch yourself identifying with this negative thought, stop yourself immediately. At that exact moment, replace the negative thought with an affirmation, such as "I share the divine intelligence and mind that created all things, therefore, I cannot be anything else but brilliant."

By declaring, or affirming what is true, you penetrate through the shadows of doubt and fear. By speaking the truth, the lies begin to fall away until you are free and unburdened by the false beliefs that had limited your true potential. Instantly, the confusion lifts and you begin to feel lighter as you recall your true greatness. If you suffered a great deal in the past, it may take more practice and patience to get rid of your false beliefs, but keep at it. If you practice daily; you will certainly be able to obtain the results you seek. Don't allow yourself to get distracted by the demands of the busy day. Don't allow any excuse to pull your attention away from your commitment to being mindful.

Focusing on yourself does not make you selfish. Indeed, nothing is more important than your happiness and the best way to help others is to first make sure that you are happy yourself. If you are normally a person who is a 'giver' or 'people pleaser' you probably have a loooong way to go before you could reasonably be considered selfish. If selfishness and self-sacrifice are on a continuum, many people I counsel are way over on the self-sacrifice side that says "I don't matter," "Everyone else is more important," and "I just want to make others happy." If this is you, you likely need a healthy dose of self-love and self-care before you are even at a balanced state of self-love and care for others.

If you feel that you are always giving and others are always taking from you, it is likely that you can come to feel resentful. This sense of resentment should serve as a red flag. People can either give from their 'overflow' or from their sense of lack and limitation. People who give from their overflow, tend to feel light and happy when they give. They give because they have more than plenty for themselves and they wish to share their good fortune with others. People who give what they don't have feel resentful because they don't recognize that they are giving *specifically to receive something they feel they are lacking.*

For example, some people are able to cover their partner's financial expenses because they just want their partner to love them in return. This is not giving from overflow, but from lack. One person gives money expecting to receive love and finds herself, instead, feeling taken advantage of. If you are feeling unhappy, in fact, your unhappiness in life is directly tied to your beliefs that you don't matter. And, you will likely let others know that pleasing them is more important to you than feeling that sense of personal love and self-care. You NEED to bring more love to your own life. You NEED to love yourself. It is time! For only when you engage in more self-love will you finally begin to experience true joy in your life.

Each chapter ends with an Affirmation and Journaling exercise. However, prior to starting your week of Affirmations, make sure that you have read Chapters 1 and 2 of this book and have prepared your journal with one side set for recording your day and the other side of the journal set for entries describing your thoughts and perceptions during this week. Now that you have familiarized yourself with the seven steps involved in changing a thought and/or behavior sequence, you are ready to start your week and engage the Affirmation assigned for each day.

Task: Awareness
Theme: The Beginning of a New Life

Today, the past slips away and a new, infinite awareness emerges. I awaken to a realization of my true inner self as a powerful co-creator of my reality. I release all past attachment to pain and suffering. I tune in to my inner truth, recognizing it as a powerful force of creation in my life. I let go of past limiting thoughts and I suspend all doubt. I recognize that I am more powerful than I had imagined. Although my eyes may not yet be able to see what my heart already perceives, I trust that my good fortune awaits me. Today, I am able to see past my pain, fear and suffering. Beyond all doubt, I am able to see inside my true self and I recognize this true self as a union with the eternal source of all love and creation. In this realization and through this Affirmation of my true self, I am renewed.

MEDITATION
Going Deeper: General Guidelines for Meditation

Before you get started, find a sacred place. A sacred place is your quiet space where you cannot be bothered by anyone. This is YOUR space. In this sacred place, there are no phones, no children, and no distractions or demands pulling at you. If your house is full of activity and you cannot find a quiet place, go outside or go to your car; but find a personal and quiet place where you may be able to sit still for fifteen minutes.

Find a comfortable chair or place to sit and get settled in.
Make sure your feet are firmly planted on the floor. Take at least
three deep breaths, inhaling through your nose and exhaling
through your mouth. Read the Affirmation for the day out loud.
Allow the words to fill your ears and to rest in your heart. Close
your eyes and take another deep breath as you allow the words
to settle. Open your eyes and read the affirmation out loud
once more.

Sit up straight. Imagine that there is a string attached to
your head and it is holding you up. You are solid and firm, like a
mountain. Place your hands with the palm facing up as if you are
ready to receive all the goodness that the universe has in store
for you. Take a deep breath, as deep as you can. Fill your lungs
and stomach with air. Breathe in through your nose. Imagine you
are breathing in all the goodness, joy and peace that await you.
When you have filled your chest and stomach with air, try to
hold it for ten seconds. Release your breath through your mouth.
As you release your breath, imagine that you are letting go of all
that is dark and painful. Relax your entire body. Start from the
top of your head down to your toes. Relax the muscles on your
face. Relax your neck and shoulders. Relax your stomach and
back. Relax your arms and hands. Feel your buttocks and your
back pressed against the chair. Relax your legs and thighs. Feel
your feet planted firmly on the ground.

Keep your mind clear of any thought. At first, you may find
it difficult to keep your mind clear, but don't give up. If you have

trouble keeping your mind clear, focus on your breath. Feel the air caress your nostrils as you fill your lungs with air. As you exhale, focus on the air as it caresses your lips on its way out. You may actually count the breaths if you need to keep your mind occupied. If a thought enters your mind, don't get discouraged. Recognize the thought and let it go and then return to your clear state of mind. Practice this quiet meditation for fifteen minutes, two times a day. If at first you cannot sit still for fifteen minutes, do what you can and build up to the fifteen-minute point.

3. JOURNALING EXERCISE

Are you Awakening? Is your life changing in the direction of your soul's desire? The best person to judge whether you are changing or not, has got to be yourself. It is important to allow yourself enough distance from your own story to be able to see patterns of thought and behavior that you have missed in the past because you have been so attached to your story.

In the past, your reactions and attachment to your version of your life story gave you some reward for thinking and behaving as you did, but the rewarded behavior stops serving its purpose and becomes a hindrance to greater growth. Over time these thoughts and behaviors become rigid patterns that don't allow new insights to emerge. You have to be willing to ask yourself difficult questions. You must also have the courage to answer those tough questions honestly and without attachment to the emotions and feelings that emerge from your sincere responses. And the only way to do that is through questions, which you ask of yourself and then answer honestly.

The Journaling Exercise outlined at the end of each chapter provides you with questions to reflect on and answer in your journal. It must be reiterated that it is not enough to merely think about these questions and the answers, but to actually write out the question and the answers AND your thoughts about the answers. It is only by getting the thoughts out of your head that you can actually see and truly assess what you truly do think and believe. But as long as your thoughts, worries, dreams, and fears stay in your head, they will remain a confusing and overwhelming jumble which only adds to your frustration and unhappiness. The reason why people seek therapist's or psychologist's guidance is to help them gain some sense of perspective and distance from their own story, which is precisely what you are doing when you journal. It's therapy without the bill.

A. Finding Where You Are Blocked

In your journal, write out your answers to these questions as best you are able. Even if you don't know the exact answer, it is good to write out what the answers might be, and then feel which answer feels right inside and on your skin. More often than not, this is the response that is truest to who you really are. Again, the goal is to begin to learn how to hear your own voice, and this is best done not by listening, per se, but by 'knowing' if something feels right and feels true. It is important to begin pushing back all the voices in your head (of friends, family, clergy, teachers, etc) who want to tell you how to live your life, and begin feeling for the truth of who YOU really are and how YOU want to spend your life. This is done by allowing what feels right to bubble up from within.

1. Do you feel that you are living your life to your fullest potential?

2. If not, do you know what is blocking your growth?

3. If you don't know what is blocking or limiting you, take a moment and check in with your body.

   a. Then, ask yourself, "What is blocking me?"

   b. Close your eyes and focus all your attention in you body. Is there a place in your body where you are feeling tension or tightness? Perhaps your stomach feels upset or your shoulders tense. Now ask yourself, if that stress or tension reminds you of any experience from your past.

   c. If so, write down that experience in your journal. Although you may not automatically connect your body's tension with a blocked emotion or barrier, as you write down your experience, you will begin to forge other connections to events and experiences that have happened in your life. If you are not able to immediately identify what is blocking you, don't despair, there will be plenty of time to identify these patterns as you move through the various exercises in the book. You have already begun your search and have opened the door to your inner awareness. Once this door is opened, you can't close it again. You will begin to see that memories and events become increasingly more apparent and you will begin to see patterns emerging.

B. Setting a Baseline

In order for you to know whether your efforts are paying off, you must have some way of measuring your change. To measure progress, you must have at least two points of assessment, such as a beginning and end, or a before and after. Before you get started on your week of transformation, you need to establish a baseline so that you are able to measure your growth and progress at the end of the week. A baseline measurement starts with an assessment of your current situation. At the end of the week, you will take a second measure and compare that measure to the first to see how much you've grown. You can continue to implement the exercises in subsequent weeks, after you complete the Week of Awakening in order to expand your growth. Be sure to always establish your baseline (pre-test) and to assess your progress at the end of your allotted time.

Psychologists like to use a very simple tool, called a 'Likert Scale,' because they are easy to understand and use. Below is an example of a Likert scale:

$$1—2—3—4—5—6—7—8—9—10$$

Least/Little   **Much/Most**

Scoring a particular question with a '1' means you are not at all satisfied. A 10 means you are very satisfied with regard to that particular question. So, when presented with a question or statement, give yourself a rating that describes how you feel right now. Write this number down in your journal and leave it alone until the end of the week when you will come back to it to evaluate your progress. By doing so, you have established your 'baseline.' This baseline number will serve as your 'before' measure. At the end of the week, when you have completed your program, you will come back to that 'before' score and you will rate yourself again to determine your 'after' score, and therefore the progress you have made during the week. Copy the questions below onto the first page and the last page of your journal.

Assessment Questions

(Questions preceded by a number: respond on the Likert Scale. Questions preceded by a letter: write out as a Journaling Exercise.)

1. Do I care for my mind? (Respond using the Likert Scale)

    a. In what ways can I better care for my mind? (Journaling exercise)

2. Do I care for my body? (Likert)

    a. In what ways can I better care for my body? (Journal)

3. Do I care for my spirit?

    a. In what ways can I better care for my spirit – my sense of self-love?

4. Am I content and joyful for my life as it is right now?

    a. What is one small change I would love to permanently make to my life?

b. What is the biggest thing in my life that I wish to change?

c. What are the 10 things, people, places, or experiences I know I do NOT want in my life anymore? In other words, what are the sources of negative energy in my life that I know I must remove, or push away from, if I am ever going to discover my happiness?

5. Am I certain that I am living my unique purpose and to my potential?

a. What do I believe my true life purpose is?

b. If I don't know, I will allow myself to speculate and ask "What MIGHT it be?" What are three things I've often thought would bring me great joy to be doing more of?

c. What could I do that would bring me the greatest joy to be doing with in my life?

d. Do I have the courage to begin living a new life by of doing what I love to do, knowing that what I love to do consists of my life's purpose?

6. Do I know what I need in order to make the necessary changes in my life?

a. What do I need to have, do, or say in order to change my life NOW?

7. Rather than sitting and waiting for change to take place, am I doing what I can to implement the changes I wish to see?

a. If not, what is holding me back?

b. What am I most afraid of?

c. Do I have the courage to pass through my fear?

d. Do I want a NEW life and NEW joy badly enough to be willing to confront what I most fear, and then push through my fears, even though my knees may be shaking?

Going Deeper

Write in your journal these questions and the answers to them:

1. What were you surprised by in the previous Journaling Exercises?

    a. Why were you surprised?

2. What parts of the Journaling Exercises did you enjoy?

3. Sometimes questions give rise to new questions. What further questions came to you as you were answering those in today's Journaling Exercise? Take time to write those questions out again, speculating/playing with what the answers might be. Don't worry about being exact. The more you tinker with it, the more you will eventually get a feel for what answer rings true for you.

One Note Regarding Journaling

At times journaling can seem silly or even pointless. You may think, "It's just words on paper. What good is journaling?" By answering questions about ourselves and putting those answers on paper, we have the ability to look at our answers and, thus, ourselves objectively. It's like looking at the x-ray of a broken leg, rather than just staring at your broken leg and wondering what's wrong. Journaling helps us to look from the outside at our problems, and to see what is really going on. And, more often than not, just looking deeply at our own problems has the capacity to change our lives. It really is that powerful of a thing to do.

It may sound crazy, but it's true. We are powerful, divine beings and often become distracted by our fears, insecurities and pains that we have endured. Just seeing who we really are can have a powerfully transformative effect on our lives and attitudes. Journaling has the effect of basically being a doctor to ourselves, and it is so simple. You don't have to be some great writer because only you will ever need to read your journal. It is just a tool for helping you better understand yourself.

4

DAY 2: IDENTIFICATION: NAMING YOUR MONSTERS

"¿Eres? ¿O te haces?"[20]

...Grandmother Lidia

The second step in changing unhealthy patterns is being able to put a name to what scares or limits you. There is much to be gained by being able to identify and break limiting patterns of fear and pain that keep re-appearing in our lives.

Our native ancestors believed that the journey of life and our ever-expanding awareness represent an eternal journey of the soul, which unfolds in predictable and measurable cycles. We can examine the cycles of life which occur all around us and learn by observing their natural rhythms. By observing the cycles in nature, we learn that the best time to plant is in the spring and that the harvest comes in the fall. We measure life in predictable

---

20   *"Are you? Or do you pretend?"*

cycles that are either brief or long. An hour is a cycle measured in 60 minutes while a year is measured in 365 days.

The same approach can be applied to identify damaging patterns of thoughts and behaviors which occur in our lives. Very often we are not aware that we are feeding and maintaining these limiting and damaging patterns because we are too engrossed in living them. We tend to become so entangled by the pain and drama of our life that we lose perspective, and we lose the ability to see with objectivity. As the saying goes, "You can't see the forest for the trees."

We tend to attach ourselves to and get so wrapped up in our version of reality and to the stories of pain and injury that we have constructed to define our existence, no matter how limiting and harmful these personal stories might be. Our egos become too entangled in the drama of our lives. As we get pulled by these strong emotions, we become unable to notice the patterns that develop. This is what it means to fall asleep – to lose true connection to a conscious and deliberate life that flows from your center and source of strength. When you learn to step back and see your life from a place of curious detachment, you will be able to see how your thoughts and behaviors have created predictable patterns that have emerged. You know you are finally living deliberately when you can see the patterns you have been re-creating and reliving. Once you learn how to identify these patterns, you can create a plan of action.

Five Palm Trees

Along the side of my driveway, I have planted five palm trees. Three of these palm trees have grown strong and tall while two have become entangled by the morning glory vines that have wrapped themselves around the base of the trunks. Last year, I was able to cut the vines around the palm trees, trying to free them from the choking hold of the vines. Today, the two palm trees are taller than last year, but still are not as tall as the first three trees that grew without being restricted. Just like the palm trees, our pain and suffering sometimes wrap themselves around our souls (*tonalli*) and begin to limit our potential for growth.

Our minds are constantly calculating and making assumptions and interpretations about what is happening around us. We judge whether someone likes us or not based on our recollections, perceptions and emotions. We form impressions and make predictions about the future based on our experiences of the past. We are constantly projecting and interpreting messages from our environment which we construct based on the experiences, emotions, and memories that we have lived. Yet, our perceptions are limited by our individual experiences of reality. We can't perceive another perspective or reality because we have no other experience of life other than our very own. Because we are still thinking about and trying to understand why and how it was that we suffered as much as we did, everyone and everything we see we perceive through our past pain. Suddenly it seems that we have not escaped, evolved or changed, because we seem to perceive only pain. The experiences of pain, lack and suffering from a past long gone can become reintroduced in our lives without our conscious awareness. These experiences are like the vines choking my palm trees. They hold us down, stunt our growth, and keep us from our destiny.

By now, I have lived long enough to notice repetitive patterns and cycles that occur in my own life. I have learned to break these limiting patterns in order to free myself of their grip. I am neither the smartest person, nor am I the fastest learner in the world. My personal journey has been marked by great success but also by many pitfalls and failures. My whole purpose for including my personal journey in each chapter is to illustrate that I have been where you are. I have lived the lie, the false life. I know what it is to live in a long slumber of unfulfillment, chasing things and dreams that really are not you. I KNOW THAT LIFE! And I also know what it's like to finally WAKE UP! The purpose of this book is to share with you my own journey of Awakening, and through personal and clinical experience guide you as you continue on your own journey.

In many ways, I have learned so much more from my perceived mistakes than from my successes. I developed the process that is outlined in this book, as a result of my personal and professional work and the experiences that I have gathered along the way. I continue to personally practice this approach and I also teach this method of change to my clients.

If you are feeling stuck and discouraged, I know that this method will help you break through the perceived barriers and limiting cycles that are impeding you. The simple formula outlined in this book will be instrumental in helping you to AWAKEN to your true potential and greatest joy, life *your* life, and become the person you were always intended to be.

*"No te dejes arrastrar ni por los buenos, ni por los malos,
que mañana cambian de lugar."*[21]

...Grandmother Lidia

Emotional Intelligence

Once you become aware that you are entertaining unhealthy thoughts and behavior patterns, the second step in this process of Awakening is to develop the appropriate vocabulary to accurately describe what is happening to you. Developing the vocabulary required to accurately express feelings is called emotional intelligence. Being able to adequately describe and define our

21 *"Don't allow yourself to be dragged either by those that are good or by those who are bad, for tomorrow they will switch sides."* Do not judge your friends or enemies. One day you may find that your friend is now your enemy and your enemy is now your friend.

emotional reactions is not a skill we are born with. Quite the contrary, in many cultures, boys are taught that expressing emotion is a sign of weakness and 'sentimentality.' Girls are taught that expressing emotions make them hysterical or overly vulnerable. What we don't realize is that by teaching children not to appreciate and express their emotions we are actually decreasing their ability to survive, adapt, and find true happiness.

Growing up, you might have been taught to keep the pain to yourself; not to cry or express weakness. As a result, over time, you may have developed a certain numbness. For example, you may have some general sense that something is wrong, but perhaps you never developed the emotional vocabulary to express what is happening to you. Without the proper label, our experiences can hide and can find other 'bad emotions' to join. These bad emotions hang out in a clump; an ill-defined mess of pain. We don't label these subtle and different perceptions because we are afraid of getting near them. We fear getting so close that we will be sucked in by them and won't be able to survive their pull. Pretty soon, all you know is that you feel bad, but you may not be able to tell the difference between feelings of sadness, hurt, betrayal, etc. What you know for certain is that it all just feels bad.

"No hay mal que dure para siempre." [22]

…Grandmother Lidia

---

22   *"There is no harm that can last forever."*

Learning to 'name your monsters' is a critical step towards being able to combat and defeat them. Your words are powerful. They have the ability to manifest what is spoken, as well as to destroy what is not true. When you learn to properly label your emotional experiences, you can develop a certain distance or detachment from the emotion. You can say for example, "There is that feeling of sadness that I am experiencing right now." That is a more useful reaction than identifying yourself with the sadness. ("I AM sad" basically means my identity IS sadness, instead of saying I am EXPERIENCING sadness – i.e the sadness is not my identity but just another life experience that will soon pass.) With certain detachment you do not have to let the sadness drag you down. Soon, with the power of labels and naming, you recognize that your emotions don't define you. The painful emotions and feelings come and the happy ones leave, just as easily. These transitory emotions in no way define your true identity. You are not defined by the scars you endure, and no person or circumstance from your past has the ability to control or define you.

Learning to properly label your emotional reactions allows you to experience mastery and control over them. You don't want to become a robot with no feelings and emotions. That would take away a great deal of the beauty, flavor and complexity of life. But you don't have to be dragged down by your emotions, either. By learning to properly label what is limiting or hurting you, you can choose not to get too attached to what you recognize to be a passing moment and you can begin to develop a plan of action to combat against your pain and the barriers to your greater growth.

One way to become more aware and to learn to label your emotions is by practicing mindfulness. As mentioned earlier, mindfulness is the attentive awareness of the reality of things and experiences as they unfold and are perceived in the present moment. It is a powerful tool to fight against delusion because it allows us to perceive our reality without attaching our emotions and reactions.

By observing reality as it unfolds, we become more capable of understanding everything that is taking place. By staying focused on the here and now, you become more aware of your body's functions, your breathing and sensations. This increases your awareness and thus your wisdom. Practicing mindfulness is very easy. You simply maintain attention centered on your unhindered awareness – you count your breaths and faithfully return back to your point of focus whenever you become distracted by other thoughts. By staying focused on the present, either by focusing on your breathing or on maintaining a clear mind, you learn to turn down the volume on all other intruding thoughts and feelings. The result is a clear mind, unhindered by the distracting noise of irrelevant, irrational and irritating thoughts that do not add anything to your growth.

We have already learned that many of our experiences can occur just below the level of our awareness. In fact, most of our experiences occur at a subconscious level. Practicing mindfulness can help you learn to experience your feelings as they occur, so that you can adequately label these experiences and then

recognize the subconscious beliefs driving the experience.

Mindfulness practice can allow you to see yourself as you are. By learning to be present to the moment, you can begin to focus inward, paying attention to muscle tension as it expresses itself in your body.

Mindfulness allows you to focus your attention on your breathing, so that you can check to see how it changes under different emotional situations. As you experience tension and stress, do you notice your breathing becoming shallow, short or troubled?

Your body and your breathing have a quiet language all their own which can reveal great and profound insights to you, as you learn to pay attention.

Learn to Unpack Your Emotions

We tend to pack our experiences of hurt and sadness in an emotional suitcase where these experiences mix themselves with other negative experiences we've kept from years past. Soon, the emotional suitcase becomes too heavy to carry and, yet, we cannot (or choose not to) see inside that suitcase that is weighing us down. Learning to label the different items in your emotional baggage can help you determine what to keep and what to throw away so that your load is much lighter. Today, just as airlines are charging for every bag you take, it helps to travel light emotionally too, because there is a cost to our relationships and experiences when we're carrying excess emotional baggage.

As you learn to identify your emotions, you will learn that spiral downward slide of pain, depression and suffering always is triggered by some single thought or memory. What is the thought that happened just before you started down an automatic pattern of self-damaging behaviors? Maybe someone hurt your feelings or disappointed you and this disappointment started a negative chain reaction. Maybe you expected to get affection that you never received. As negative thoughts attract more negative thoughts, soon you are trapped in an endless cycle of negative thinking which pulls you down an endless spiral. If you can identify the single thought or idea that triggers your automatic chain reaction, you can prevent the entire sequence from ever taking place.

If you know that being around a certain person causes you to act in ways that are not healthy for you, you may have to decide to change your relationship to that individual and avoid the trigger altogether. Most triggers are related to a person, a place or a given situation or circumstance, but even sights or smells can be enough to trigger negative patterns. Once you are triggered, your thoughts and behaviors go through predictable patterns that are more difficult to interrupt once they are initiated. The secret is to stop these triggers before they start, which requires identifying them, first.

You must learn to identify exactly where and how you get stuck in these patterns, then you must fight against your natural tendency to be pulled by their attraction because this pull will force you to react the same old way to the same old situation. When you choose to react differently to the same circumstances that now have become fixed patterns, you will break the endless cycle that keeps you from living your true potential.

A few thoughts to consider (and perhaps journal about) as you move into the exercises for today.

- How comfortable are you labeling your emotions?

- Are you aware of the 'triggers' that pull you into a negative emotional vortex?

- Can you start practicing mindfulness and become aware of the present moment as you learn to focus on your breath and/or maintaining your mind clear of any intruding thoughts?

Day Two

Task: IDENTIFICATION

1. AFFIRMATION

Remember: The Affirmation gets read as you start your day and as you are ready for bed. The Meditation is fifteen minutes of clearing the mind. This is mindful Meditation that allows for clarity and focus. As you engage this process, you will be impacted by what you have read in the Affirmation. Insights will occur during the Meditation that provide you with valuable information based on what you have read in the Affirmation .

The Journaling Exercise consists of writing out your thoughts, feelings and reactions related to the Affirmation and Meditation that you completed for the day, as well as any other events or insights that you experienced throughout the day.

Task: Identification
Theme: Connecting to Your Inner Truth

Even when the next step in my life seems uncertain, I know that a greater intelligence than mine holds all things together. As I shine the light of my true self on my fears, I am able to identify all obstacles in my way. I can see where I have fallen short of my true self. Rather than punish myself, I delight in my ability to identify my fears and I commit to chase these away. I do not allow worry and stress to dominate my life. I let go and I trust that a loving intelligence is eternally guiding my journey. I keep constant watch over my thoughts and I repudiate all fears and doubts that threaten my single -minded resolve. I will not allow uncertainty to threaten my progress. I know that all experience of pain and stress is but a changing condition. Always, at the center of truth is the light of love that illuminates my path. I know that there is a Universal Law that acts upon my thoughts. I there-fore imagine my life filled with all the peace and goodness the universe provides. I know that I am a divine creation and that all goodness flows to me. There is nothing I can do to interfere with this divine flow. I open my heart and my hands and willingly receive the goodness that is rightfully mine.

1. MEDITATION

(Go back to Chapter 3 and read the general format for your Meditation before starting.)

2. JOURNALING EXERCISE

Step 1: (This exercise is described in greater detail in my first book, *The Promise of the Fifth Sun.*)

Write down your life story.

As you write your life story, pay extra close attention to the first 7 to 9 years of your life because these early years are your 'formative years.' These are the years when the basis of your personality is being established. Most often, everything else in life becomes a way for us to try and resolve the early patterns that were set in motion. Focus on writing your story in increments of five years, as sketched out below:

- 0 to 5 years: Write down everything that you remember as well as what you have heard about yourself from others. You may not actually remember this part of your childhood, but you have surely heard from your parents stories of when you were a baby. What type of baby, toddler, and young child were you?

- 5-10: What do you remember? Where did you live? What games did you play? What special events do you recall? Particular memories? Who were your friends? What did you play?

- 10-15: What do you recall about school and friendships? How did you get along with your siblings and parents? What else do you remember? Did you have a boyfriend/girlfriend? What do you remember about this person and your experiences of dating?

Continue through all five-year segments, up to your present age. Take your time writing your story. The more detail that you can recall, the better. Some people have blocked a great portion of their childhood and life from memory. If this is your case, write down as much as you can and also describe what was happening with your family. Where were you living? What challenges was your family encountering? Write down other memories that you have gathered. Don't worry if you don't remember every last detail; just write what you remember, as fully as you can.

Finish writing your story until you get right to the present and then leave it alone for a couple of days. Go back and read your story to yourself. Pick a highlighter and outline all of the 'themes' that you are able to identify. See how these patterns repeat throughout.

1. What patterns do you see emerging? Write down the patterns that you have observed on a separate sheet of paper. What do these patterns show you?

2. What are your thoughts and feelings as you are doing this exercise?

3. What is the general tone of your story? Is it a tragic story? Are you victimized?

4. What false teachings, or false beliefs, were incorporated into these old patterns?

5. What are the lessons that you have learned along the way?

6. Who taught you that false lesson?

7. Why did you hold on to that lesson until now?

Read back to yourself what you wrote. Outline the common themes and repetitive patterns you are able to identify The answers to these questions begin to outline your life script. Whether you are aware of it or not, these repetitive themes have become your map of life. *These are the conflicts and challenges that continue to repeat in your life because they are looking for resolution. Your mind will not tolerate a mystery that is not resolved.* If you are feeling as though you are attracting the same type of relationship in your life, or that people are always taking advantage of you or that life is not fair, etc., these are all signs that you have fallen into a repetitive pattern that must be broken. Write down these repetitive patterns separately.

Step 2:

Next, become aware of how, where and when these false beliefs still occur in your life. As you become aware, take a moment and pay attention to your mind and body's reaction.

1. Where in your body are you experiencing tightness and discomfort?

2. What thought is triggering your reaction?

3. Can you isolate and examine the troubling thought?

Be careful not to allow yourself to be carried away by the pull of those negative thoughts. You want to become familiar with the thoughts as they begin to emerge. Don't allow your old patterns of thoughts and behaviors to take over your reactions because once they do, there may be little you can do to stop the sequence of automatic reactions that follow. You CAN stop an automatic thought or behavior pattern just before it triggers an automatic sequence response. You CAN render these thoughts ineffective and stop them from pulling you into the old ways of being. As you gain experience, you will be able to more easily identify the automatic thoughts that trigger you. You will be able to interrupt these automatic sequences and eventually destroy them.

5

DAY 3: INTERRUPTION: ALTERING THE HARD-DRIVE

"En esta vida, todos estamos de pasada,
escogiendo y recogiendo de lo que nos
servirá para la eternidad."[23]

...Grandmother Lidia

As the oldest child in my family, I grew up trying my best to be a substitute father, protector and provider to my brothers. I had to ensure the safety of my brothers and my mother, because my father drank heavily and often. As a result, I had to grow up fast. Somehow, along the way, I learned that the usual rules and guidelines, which people employed to live their lives, just didn't apply for my family and me. We had to work harder and be extra resourceful in order to address the many chaotic emergencies that regularly emerged. In order to escape the extreme poverty

---

23   *"In this life, we are all just passing by, choosing and gathering what will serve us for eternity."*

that surrounded my family, I felt I had to take big risks and go as far as possible and achieve as much as possible in order to provide a different reality for my family and me. I desperately longed to create a different life than the one I had lived. I was always searching for the escape door to transport me into the life of joy, peace and success that I knew waited for me far from the chaos of my home.

About ten years ago, in my thirties, I made a decision to move far away from home and my family for the first time in my life. I wanted to feel free to give voice to an inner longing I had felt, since childhood, but which I could not define. It was as though I was responding to some inner call. It was, I would discover later, the very voice I had silenced as an 11 year-old being scolded by his mother, and vowing to never let that happen again. It was the voice of my own soul – my *tonalli* – surging up from within, refusing to be quiet anymore. It was the voice of my soul refusing to be numb and asleep anymore.

I was INTERRUPTING my life as I knew it to begin a new journey in a new direction. I didn't know where life was taking me. I only knew three things:

1. My old life just didn't work for me and for my soul anymore; and
2. I was on a quest for deeper guidance, searching for a connection to the greater mystery of life, and desiring to gain a more meaningful understanding that would compensate for a childhood of chaos and uncertainty;

3. I was still in the grip of the sleep, still hunting for
   success, still seeking approval.

In the end, what I was really searching for was the happiness
that had eluded me for decades. It was the happiness and fulfillment that cannot happen when a soul is asleep. I longed to have
my joy rise up from within. And now, it had begun by the simple
act of geographically leaving behind 'what was,' even though I
still was driven by many of the beliefs of my past. I was about
to enter a great period of 'sorting out' who I was to become and
shed who I know longer was.

Fresh out of graduate school and armed with my doctorate
in hand, I felt there was nothing I couldn't do. At some point,
I told myself I would go out into the world and find my fame
and fortune. I would make lots of money and buy my parents a
house and help my brothers and sister whenever they needed my
support. Somehow, I was convinced my destiny waited for me
far from my family and home, far from the safety of what I had
known and the familiarity of my environment. Far away, there
must be some destination that would wipe away and purify the
suffering my family endured.

"El presumido presume mas sobre lo que no tiene."[24]

...Grandmother Lidia

---

24   *"The boastful person brags most of having what he is
most lacking."*

I felt ready to conquer the world. Not that I was lacking anything, quite the contrary. I felt I had the Midas touch and I kept reaping success after success. Yet, I was never content and so I was constantly feeling restless and unsatisfied, searching for the next promotion and the bigger prize I was convinced waited around the next corner. I didn't know it at the time, but something in me was longing to WAKE UP. I was already AWARE that I was unhappy and discontent with my life. I was going through the motions of a routine, but felt that something greater waited for me, if I were willing to venture away from my familiar surroundings.

I had also IDENTIFIED limiting patterns and elements of my life, one was that I still defined my life by all my responsibilities in Chicago. I knew that the very life I had been living for almost 35 years was no longer mine and had to be INTERRUPTED. Something had to change. I had become dead inside.

How We Fall Asleep

Negative thoughts and false lessons become recorded and integrated in our minds with everything else that we have learned. During the first 7 to 9 years of our lives, we are creating what comes to be known as our personality. We watch our parents and learn about love and loss by watching their interactions with us and with each other. Our parents show us by their love and affection that we are valuable. The love of our parents feels good, because it reminds us of a universal comfort, a familiar and cherished feeling of safety, power and peace.

Sometimes, during the formative years, children are exposed to serious pain, abuse and mistreatment. These early experiences of pain can become engrained in the base of the personality. "You are worthless." "It's your fault." "You are a sinner." These are all false lessons that are often taught repeatedly to children. Over time, these false lessons become part of the hard drive of the personality. Your true voice, your *tonalli*, your soul, your true self always knows that these lessons are not true. But, often, as you grow, you can doubt the value and truth of your own inner voice. Your inner voice always seeks to communicate with you through gut feelings and an inner voice that makes you say, "Something told me to..." But if you doubt that you are a part of the Universal Mind of the Creator, you can dismiss these intuitive messages. You miss these intuitive messages long enough and you can begin to feel as though you are living your life asleep, having forgotten about your true identity and power.

It is never too late to stop yourself from entertaining a negative thought. One way to interrupt a negative thought once it starts is to ask yourself this question, "Is this thought coming from my ego and fear? Or is this thought coming from my higher sense of self-awareness?" Does the thought bring anxiety and trepidation, or peace and aliveness?

Let the question bounce around inside you and let it create a physical reaction. Do you feel upbeat and exhilarated or do you feel tension? If you feel tension, where and how does your body register it? If you feel upbeat, most likely you are responding from your higher sense of self awareness.

The goal in hearing your inner voice – your intuition – is to learn to read your body. It is to learn to feel the answer. How something feels, the sensation it creates on and in your body is the primary indicator of what your intuition is saying. Intuition is not a 'thought.' It's a 'feel.' And the goal is to tune in, more and more, to the feel, the messages, and the responses of your body; for it is the communicator of your soul.

Visualization

Thoughts of fear and limitation tend to come from the ego. If you stop and breathe for a moment, you can interrupt these fears and stop them from overtaking you. You can center yourself to hear the voice of your higher self seeking to guide you through what feels right on and in your body.

Another way to interrupt a negative pattern is to employ **visualization.** Visualization is an incredible tool to help your mind create a map to your higher self. The clearer your vision is the greater likelihood that your mind will be able to manifest the desired outcome. Visualization is simple.

First, imagine a problem or situation for which you would like to receive guidance from your higher self. Clear your mind of any thought or concern. Close your eyes. Take a few deep breaths and relax. Pay attention to images as they begin to appear. Don't try to guide or direct your mind, just let the images come on their own. Your visioning might start as an isolated image, a spot of light, a color, or some specific memory. Focus your attention at the center of the emerging image and follow it. You might notice that the image begins to expand itself. Let your attention follow the vision as it unfolds. Allow yourself to be guided by the images that come to you. You will see that your vision will provide you valuable clues and the guidance you seek. You can use visualization to reverse harmful effects of the past as well as to create a better future.

If, for example, someone insults you and you react by getting angry and upset, you might want to visualize how you might have reacted differently. Try to picture the person as they insult you. How do you usually react? What bothers you most? Is it their words? Is it their facial expression? Do you think their insults are valid? Now try to imagine how you usually react. What is the trigger that gets you going? Picture how you would rather handle a similar situation in the future. Think of a response or something you would like to say that allows you to maintain your composure. By rehearsing these scenarios before they occur, you are reducing the likelihood of responding impulsively. By visualizing and projecting yourself into the various situations before they take place, you will reduce your tendency to be affected in the same old way.

Although you might have learned patterns of thought and behaviors that are unhealthy and limiting, your true potential is never truly diminished. All you need to do is learn to identify, remove and reintegrate new patterns of thoughts and behaviors. Learning to listen to your intuitive voice can undo any false lessons that you might have picked up along the way. Tools that can help you in the process of awakening include maintaining a focus on the here and now, practicing mindful meditation and visualization. With these tools you can remove limiting and unhealthy patterns and integrate new, healthier thoughts and behaviors.

Day Three

Task: INTERRUPTION – Altering the Hard Drive

1. AFFIRMATION
Theme: Holding on to the Light and the Dream

I am in control of my thoughts. The negative pulls of darkness and fear no longer control me. I have the power to interrupt all thoughts and behaviors which are incongruent to my joy. Above all things and despite all challenges, I hold on to my faith. I keep my goals and desires at the forefront of my awareness. I am ever vigilant of my thoughts, protecting my mind from the shadows of doubt. I repudiate all thoughts of lack and suffering and I fight the fears that have kept me down. I create a clear vision of my heart and soul's desire. I know that what my mind can see goes out into the Universal Law of creation. I know this law takes direction from my thoughts and begins to construct and manifest according to my vision. I hold firmly and clearly to the picture of my most cherished desires. I recognize my dream becoming a reality and I give thanks for the giving force of creation which follows my command. I watch with unbound delight as my most cherished dreams and aspirations manifest right before my very eyes.

2. MEDITATION

3. JOURNALING EXERCISE

1. Go back to your life story and write down the repetitive themes you've identified.

2. What things do you see happening in more than one of the 5-year age brackets?

3. What similar actions do you see? Similar behaviors? Similar thought patterns happening, again and again?

4. What feelings are you holding on to that don't allow you to release this pattern from your life?

5. What are you afraid of? It's okay to be afraid. When it comes to our inner lives and feelings, we all have fears. Admitting those fears, even just to ourselves, is sometimes the most powerful piece of our own transformation. Admitting fears gives us permission to recognize and accept that we have some work to do. Fears point the way to the work that is needed.

6. What do you fear would happen if you let go of this pattern?

7. What do you need to express that you have not expressed prior to now?

8. Is there something you need express to another person?

9. Is there something you need to express TO YOURSELF?

10. What actions will you take now that are different from the actions you have traditionally taken?

6

DAY 4: INCORPORATION: MOVING INTO ACTION

"El opresor vive hasta cuando se decida el oprimido."[25]

...Grandmother Lidia

As I prepared to make my cross country move, well over a decade ago, my family and friends had gathered together to celebrate my birthday and my transition. We had Mariachis playing in the living room and my brother Carlos was the DJ. Everyone had a great time. In the early hours of the following morning, my mother called with the news that my grandmother had passed away in Mexico. It took me a while to understand

---

25 *"The oppressor lives, until the oppressed decides."* We have more power than we imagine. We possess the power to stand up against forces that oppress us or hold us down. Most interestingly, the most powerful forces that keep us asleep and living the lies are the forces of thought and long-held beliefs in our own minds. Until we take action to deliberately change our core beliefs, we will forever be oppressed by our own mistaken beliefs.

exactly what had happened. *"Se nos fue. Se nos fue,"*[26] my mother kept repeating, as though my grandmother had abandoned us and run away from home.

Throughout my life, my grandmother's teachings reminded me of the existence of a universe governed by invisible forces. She taught me that reality is not the material manifestation we see, but the sacred mystery behind the observable. Now, as these lessons replayed in my mind, I wondered about their significance and meaning once again. Amidst the fear and confusion, I kept telling myself,

"Reality is beyond what I can see and feel."

Yet, I could not help but wonder, as I prepared to make my own transition, what lay ahead for me in a far-away land. I would make the journey without the physical presence of my grandmother to guide me.

The night before my grandmother's passing, I had enjoyed my birthday with friends and family, and a celebration of a new beginning. At the same time I was starting a new chapter of my life, I also had to say goodbye to one of the most influential people in my life. I was moving across the country to live and work in a place I had never seen before and where I did not know a single person. I suddenly felt abandoned, once again,

---

26   *"She left us! She left us!"*

like that child I was many years ago, left to fend in the world alone, unprotected and unfamiliar, exposed to a different reality existing outside the protective environment of a loving home. This time, however, I was choosing the experience of leaving. When my grandmother died, I could not imagine my life without her support. I could not appreciate the irony of leaving home to search a distant land for belonging. I rationalized leaving family and friends, assuring myself that I was being propelled by a deeper search for connection to myself.

I had put into motion a journey of self-discovery that would involve venturing out alone, without the guidance of Grandmother Lidia, who was my *madrina*[27] and spiritual teacher. I was not ready to face the fact that my grandmother was gone. That evening, I had an unmistakable sense of my grandmother's presence, assuring me that I needed to stay on schedule and make my cross country trip. I didn't fly to Mexico to attend her funeral. I chose instead to move to California and start my new life on time.

Not prepared to accept my grandmother's death, I felt I had not learned all that I needed to learn from this incredible woman. I could not imagine my life without her support. My grandmother made it clear to me that she would always be with me. Perhaps the fact that I was not present at her funeral has influenced her ever presence in my life since then. Regardless, I knew that making my new move in life was exactly what I needed to do.

---

27   *Godmother.*

I felt assured and strong inside. I knew this was the next step on my spiritual journey.

When I first arrived in the San Francisco Bay Area, I didn't know a single person. The world opened up to me in wonderful and frightening ways. Far away from my family and the world I once knew as familiar and comfortable, I often experienced loneliness, uncertainty, disappointment and fear. There were also incredibly giving and loving people that were available and supportive, giving me their hearts and friendship.

Looking back, I now am able to see that I often failed to reciprocate this love and affection. I was so focused on being careful not to be hurt or be betrayed that I could not fully receive the love that was so freely offered without being suspicious and mistrustful. Yet, during the ten years I lived in California, I often felt my Grandmother Lidia's presence, giving me the strength and guidance I needed to confront life's darkest moments. She often whispered her wisdom in my ear particularly in times of challenge and strife.

"El estudiante aprende solo lo que el maestro sabe." [28]

...Grandmother Lidia

---

28 *"The student learns only what the teacher knows."* Choose your teachers and mentors wisely. Be fully aware of what you are learning and who you are learning from.

She was an intensely loving woman with an intuitive power able to see through the heart and soul of any person. Strong and passionate, she was able to raise eight children alone in Mexico, while her husband worked the fields of California to send money to feed and clothe the entire family. Today, my grandmother's spirit continues to guide me and influences my personal and professional development. There is no question that she lives on in me, just as her ancestors lived on in her. Each of us carries and delivers the message of healing and AWAKENING that is provided to all by the powerful Spirit of the Universe.

Moving Into Action

Now that you've learned to identify the thoughts and behaviors that don't serve you, the next step involves moving into action. Just as I knew I had to move to California, you are being called to action by your *tonalli*. The question is, "To what are you being called?"

At first, incorporating new thoughts and behaviors will seem unusual. You may experience a strong pull to resort back to old behaviors that, while they are less healthy or adaptive, will feel more comfortable precisely because of their familiarity. This phase tends to be the most difficult for many people.

As you start to incorporate new behaviors, notice your mental and physical reactions. You may experience feelings of stress and discomfort. You may feel awkward and vulnerable or exposed, as if others are aware of your every action. These are normal feelings that are associated with the process of integrating new behaviors. As you rehearse new behaviors, you will experience less stress until these new behaviors become part of your automatic reactions.

All negative patterns are maintained by **secondary gains**. Secondary gains are inadequate rewards which maintain unhealthy behaviors. These secondary gains keep these 'supposedly' unwanted behaviors in motion by providing some level of payoff. Examples of secondary gains include fighting with your partner because it allows you to stay open to meet someone new. Getting sick allows you to miss work. Attacking someone you love allows you to avoid personal responsibility.

Secondary gains not only keep unwanted behaviors active, they give you permission to remain asleep and avoid AWAKENED insight. Identify the secondary gain that keeps your behavior pattern in motion and you can change that behavior pattern automatically.

Behaviors are intricately and deeply connected to our thoughts. As you start to incorporate new behaviors, you will recognize that thoughts that are below your level of awareness will begin to emerge and even threaten your new behavior. You may hear critical thoughts such as, "This will never last," "This is a stupid waste of time," or "What's the point, nothing is ever going to change."

As you address these emergent thoughts, you can fight them with affirmations until you find yourself acting and thinking in accordance with your true wishes and aspirations.

For the previous day, you have focused your attention on the incorporation of new thoughts and behaviors, now it's time to learn to move into action. Think of Incorporation as trying something new on for size. You can toy with the idea of exploring new thoughts and behaviors. With these new thoughts and behaviors, you can test to see how people might react differently to you. You may begin to gain a different perspective of your life and your environment, but you are still comfortably holding on to the old ways and your old identity. By the time you are ready to move into action, you have had enough time to try out new thoughts and behaviors and you have gathered enough evidence and feedback from the world to be convinced that your temporary trial membership into a new life is actually worth a deeper commitment. You move into action by setting goals and objectives. You create a plan of action that will involve commitment and dedication.

Day Four

Task: INCORPORATION- Moving into Action

AFFIRMATION
Theme: Connecting to the Eternal Source of all Energy

I trust that the power of Creation is always available to me and that it expresses itself in everyone I meet, in everything I do, and every thought I entertain. I know that I am not alone. My mind participates in the collective intelligence of the Universal Mind and I rely on the power of creation to act upon my deepest desires. I participate as a co-creator of my life. As such, I let go of limiting thoughts and I gladly make room to incorporate those thoughts and behaviors which accurately reflect the light and power of my true self. I am not bound by any mistakes of the past. I know that I have been created in the eternal mind and, thus, I am able to use this power to manifest my thoughts. The universe opens before me and the eternal source of all creation waits for me to speak my word. With blind confidence, I release my word, knowing that the Law of Creation will manifest what is spoken. The source of my supply is endless. I turn my attention to the most peaceful and still place within me, knowing that my true self resides in this eternal home of power. There, in the stillness of the divine presence, I whisper my needs. The answer I find always says **"Yes"** to my every request.

1. MEDITATION

2. JOURNALING EXERCISE

On Day Three, you journaled about the actions that you could be taking which are different from the actions you've taken in the past. As you focus on journaling today ask yourself:

1. What have been the circumstances, people, or thoughts that have kept me from being fully who I am?

2. How have I LET people's thoughts about me or expectations of me keep me from being free, keep me from being my fullest self, or keep me from expressing the truth that is inside me?

3. What was I afraid of? What did I fear (or do I fear) would happen if I stood up to people and spoke and lived my truth?

4. Am I tired of my old life yet? Has the pain of living up to other people's expectations gotten so bad that I am finally ready to change?

5. What was the reward, recognition, acknowledgement or reaction that I was seeking that kept me attached to the fixed pattern?

6. What need within me was I looking for someone else to meet?

7. Am I prepared to meet that need myself for myself?

7

DAY 5: RELEASE:
LEARNING TO FORGIVE

...and ACTUALLY LET GO of
Resentment, Negativity, and Other Limiting Beliefs.

"Lo bueno y malo; la vida y muerte,
salud y malestar son todos frutos del pensar." [29]

...Grandmother Lidia

Throughout the ten-year period of time that I lived in California, my Grandmother Lidia's presence gave me the strength and guidance I needed to confront life's darkest moments. In moments of uncertainty, fear and doubt, it was her presence that guided and protected me.

---

29   *"Good and bad, life and death, health and illness are all fruits of thought."*

Precisely ten years after the day of my birthday when my grandmother passed, I was now living back near my hometown of Aurora, Illinois and had to travel back to California for work. Two days before my trip back to California, my Grandfather Alberto, my Grandmother Lidia's husband, had been admitted into the hospital to die. The doctors had stopped feeding him or giving him water to drink. Struggling for each breath, my grandfather laid in bed, slowly fading away. The doctors had disconnected all life support and had informed the family that he would be dying soon and that those relatives who wanted to say goodbye should do so now. I rushed to the hospital and found Grandpa's room filled with relatives standing around his bed. I sat at his bedside for a while, shocked to see the withered old shell of the strong man I had always known. I held his wrinkled hand, trying to assure him with my touch that all is well, just as it should be. Suddenly, images of this man's significance and sacrifices flashed before my eyes and I felt a deep sense of gratitude and admiration for all that he had accomplished and contributed to the lives of my family and me. I watched my grandfather struggle with such intense pain that his legs and arms curved inward in a fetal position. I thought it poetic that he was leaving this earth in the same fetal position in which he had arrived. It is painful to come into this world and it is painful to leave it.

A young female nurse walked into the room speaking her name in such a low and hurried fashion that it seemed as though she wanted to be sure no one would ask to talk to her. She took a syringe and emptied morphine into the IV drip. My grandfather had stopped eating two days before and now the family watched as he faded away. His body relaxed, giving in to the effects of the powerful pain killer surging through his body. Although all life support was removed, my grandfather was breathing normally and had a normal heart rate all day long, astounding the doctors. Even at that moment, the will and force of life was strong.

I awoke Tuesday morning and completed my morning meditation. I ran for a half-hour, had a light breakfast and went into the hospital to check on my grandfather. His breathing was shallower and his body was relaxed as though he was no longer struggling with the pain. I walked to my car and, although it was a hot day in July, I sat quietly with the windows rolled up. The July Chicago sun burned and time seemed to stand still. The birds sang their song and I could hear the distant bell of a man's ice cream cart. A squirrel stood in the middle of the sidewalk shaking its tail. As I sat in the car, sweat began to form on my forehead and throughout my body. I felt frozen as if some window had opened and I had stepped through a different reality. I contemplated the reality of my grandfather's death. Although nothing seemed to be out of place, everything felt somehow different.

Having spent those two days before my trip to California in the hospital with my grandfather, I felt a bit more comfortable going to California for my business trip. In Berkeley, California, the evening of my arrival, I tried writing for a project I was working on, but had trouble concentrating. I felt my grandfather's undeniable presence with me. I felt an unusually strong need to be with family and called around. I imagined all family members and relatives huddled together for some protective comfort in anticipation of our grandfather's imminent passing. I didn't find people waiting around for death. Every relative I called was busy living their life – tending to their children and working hard to meet all their obligations.

I found myself sitting at a coffee shop in Berkeley, CA, planning meetings and interviews. I was excited and on the cusp of what was quite possibly the professional break I had always anticipated. I was going to be interviewed about my first book, "The Promise of the Fifth Sun," by several television stations in L.A., including the number one radio show in the nation. I had arrived!

The memories of that evening ten years earlier suddenly flooded me. I saw myself partying and celebrating that birthday with my family in Chicago. I recalled feeling the promise of new and prosperous beginnings waiting for me in California. At precisely that moment, sitting in that Berkeley café, planning my interviews, my phone rang. I heard my sister's familiar voice announce. "He's gone. Grandpa Alberto just passed away. "

My grandfather was the last grandparent alive. In his 94 years of life, Don Alberto had witnessed the transformation of the world, recalling the time during WWII when he looked up at a San Francisco sky covered with war planes. Thinking it was the end of the world, Don Alberto fell to his knees and began to pray for the safety and future of his family. Now, in his passing, he was once again leading a transition for his family. My grandfather also worked and contributed to the industrial boom in Chicago. He was a *mariachi* singer and a passionate lover of life and women. Although my grandparents argued often and always about my grandfather's 'incorrigible ways,' there was an undeniable love and tenderness in their relationship and in their interactions with each other. My grandmother would giggle as if for no reason while my grandfather gave her half a smile and a wink.

As the news of my grandfather's passing began to sink in, for one second, I heard myself thinking that perhaps I would stay in California and keep my commitments, rather than return for the funeral. Just as suddenly, I recognized the same voice that rang in my ears ten years earlier, when I chose my move rather than attend my Grandmother Lidia's funeral. Then, my spiritual journey pulled me from family and with what I believed was the blessing of my grandmother. This time, my spiritual journey called me back. I knew I needed to return and be a part of this final goodbye to a generation that shaped my family and me.

My birthday, ten years earlier, marked by my grandmother's death, had also marked the beginning of my journey for self-discovery. Now, ten years later, on my birthday, my grandmother was calling me home to say goodbye to my grandfather and to close the journey by returning to the place where I began. I could not help but feel my grandmother watching over me. I could feel her standing next to me. Her arms crossed and her lips pressed together, she was waiting for my decision. Patiently, the universe had waited and orchestrated for my eyes and heart to open. If I returned, it would be to celebrate the last ten years of my life, as well as the passing from this life to eternity of a simple, magnificent and honorable man who worked, with limitations and mistakes,but with undying devotion, for the betterment of his entire family.

I cancelled all my commitments and found a flight back to Chicago. I spent most of my birthday on a plane or waiting in Phoenix for a delayed connecting flight. I rushed home from the airport, showered and put on a suit before running out the door. I arrived at the funeral home for the wake a half hour before it closed. Greeted by my parents, siblings, uncles and cousins, I felt overwhelmed with emotion. I sat in a chair in the middle of the room full of mourners. I felt my sister's hand tapping on my shoulder. She sat next to me and whispered, "Happy Birthday, brother."

Ten years later, again on my birthday, I was now given an opportunity to complete this circle, to let go, to forgive myself, to return home to rejoin my family, and to say goodbye to my grandfather as he joined my grandmother. I returned humbled and grateful for the lessons I had learned. The precious, passing perfume of life suddenly became more exquisite to me. The importance of marking life, of forging solid relationships with family and friends, began to hang over me, revealing a new

appreciation for the time we are given to express our love.
I had ventured far from home and realized there are cousins
and uncles, nephews and nieces that I have not known.

I marveled at the incredible birthday gift I was given once
again. As I was reminded of celebrating life and new Awakenings, I realized that my grandparents are still teaching me. They
are paving the way into the realm of non-physical existence. A
decade ago, when the phone call from Mexico announced my
grandmother's passing, I was celebrating my birthday and preparing to move to California to start a new life. Now, on this July
19th, I was experiencing another celebration of birth and new
life, letting go of 'what was' in order to make room to fully allow
myself to be the person I was always intended to be. I was finally
able to live my life guided fully by my intuition and my burning
passion to write, create and continue the healing work that my
Grandmother Lidia had taught me.

Even in these times of sadness and loss, the ever-loving
power and poetry of creation is orchestrating life to awaken us
to deeper levels of awareness. This was not a lamentation of
someone's death, but a celebration of abundant life, the evidence
of which could be found in every face in the crowd.

My family requested that I offer a eulogy for the funeral
Mass, the next morning. There was unmistakable electricity to
the moment, as if time itself had suddenly stopped and brought
together, the living and the dead, the young and the old. There,
in that old church, the past had intertwined itself with the present

and the future. Looking out into the crowd, I felt a profound appreciation for the one man responsible for bringing forth so many lives. All of these young college students, new families and aging grandparents owed their residency in the United States to my grandfather, who worked hard following a vision of having his family reunited. Even now, he was ensuring that we would remain together.

I thought about the resentments I've held since childhood and looked at the faces of those one or two, now aging, relatives who had harmed me when I was a child. I realized how utterly oblivious they must be about my troubled memories. If anyone does remember what suffering I endured, what does it matter decades later? The sensitivities of an injured child often survive into adulthood, but that doesn't necessarily mean they should. No child should have to suffer mistreatment, but no adult should have to live with the pain and anguish of a childhood pain that never heals. I was suddenly and painfully aware of how much time I wasted holding on to old wounds and disappointments. After Mass, I joined the long line of cars and drove to a beautiful cemetery in nearby Batavia.

Grandfather Alberto would not be buried next to Grandmother Lidia in Mexico. Modern economic crises and logistics made it impossible for his body to return home. I watched silently, as my grandfather's casket was lowered into the ground. At that moment, I felt a chill up and down my spine and the unmistakable presence of my grandmother. I heard her voice whispering this phrase in my ear:

*"La fuente de la Verdad y del poder se encuentra
en nuestra completa comunion y union con el espiritu
que trae toda materia a la percepcion.*

*Tu has sido invitado para que seas su testigo atraves
del tiempo y espacio."*[30]

...Grandmother Lidia

Just then, I looked to my left and saw a giant eagle perched on the wooden fence just feet away from me. The eagle – messenger of the heavens descending to earth and symbol of the spiritual guest that has guided the grand journey of our ancestors – perched itself to mark this moment for me. I felt a knot in my throat and recognized the unmistakable ancestor's presence honoring this sacred ground.

As if able to read my thoughts, my mother walked up to me and said, "You are lucky. Now you have both of your grandparents to watch over you from heaven." I smiled and agreed. I felt

---

30   *"The source of truth and power lies in our complete communion and union with the Spirit that brings all matter into perception. You are invited to be ITS witness in time and space."*

complete as I released the past and reaffirmed my commitment
to live my life ever mindful of the sacred messages that
continuously seek to communicate a deeper truth. These truths
are self-evident and available to any and all who are willing to
AWAKEN to the boundless power and infinite wisdom of life
as it unfolds right before our very eyes.

We have all been bombarded my messages that tell us we
must 'have it all' in order to be happy. Cars, homes, power and
titles. I have had those desires and successes. But, eventually,
they proved to be trappings and distractions from the values
I had been taught and incongruent to the true self that now
stirred within me. It was both strange and wonderful how the
letting go of my final grandparent – releasing him to the grand
Spirit of life – had the effect of bringing me back to myself.
It took letting go of those who had truly shaped me to finally
become me. It is as if their full spirit now lives on in me. I plan
to continue to honor their work and contribution, finding ways
to share the rich knowledge they entrusted to me.

Even on this day of his funeral, my grandfather had managed
to unite his family, which now is scattered all over the United
States and Mexico. I reflected on the product of my grandfather's
love and work. I thought about our modern condition and how,
for one reason or another, family and friends are often separated,
finding it increasingly more difficult to spend time together, to
socialize and show each other the support and affection that
can nurture us during the toughest times. As I looked out, I saw

the faces of those that I hadn't seen since my childhood. Some relatives I remembered had hurt me as a child, so I stayed away. Others I felt insulted by, so I stayed away. I am certain others felt hurt and insulted by me, so they must have also stayed away from me. I realized that all of us feel we have some valid reason for staying away from those we love and for logically explaining to ourselves why we hold our pain and resentment.

How often I have held my pain, distancing myself from insults, critiques offenses, indifferences, and jealousies. When I was a child, I felt I was right to stay away really from my own self, not to mention others, so that I would no longer feel pain. This day, as I looked into the beautiful and youthful faces of my nephews and nieces, cousins, uncles and friends, I realized how much we hold on to hurt feelings and memories long after anyone else has any idea or recollection of the events that have injured us so much. In times of great change, of wars and failed economies, of racial hatred and unparalleled greed and pollution, there is no more critical time than NOW to come together and heal. We must be able to recognize those thoughts that cloud our thinking and that force us to live a life of limitation and isolation.

With my grandfather's passing a cycle of life was complete and a new one began. Life had come full circle and I was now being called to lead our ancestral and familial legacy. I am called to pass on to new generations the truths of AWAKENING and TRANSFORMATION that had been passed to me.

Now, as my grandparents are united and as I reflect on my life from childhood to the present, I feel I stand at the threshold of eternity. I am able to feel my transition from young adult to mature. The temporary nature of all of our sensations must leave us all with a desire to live fully aware of the precious nature of each passing moment. I keep my heart and mind alert to receive message from the universe. The universe is forever seeking to communicate specifically to you in the form of coincidences and synchronicities. These sorts of 'coincidences' seem to multiply, the more open and receptive I become. At the exact moment of my recognition of such otherworldly communication, I feel the unmistakable presence of my grandmother still teaching me the importance of honoring this invisible, creative and healing power at the center of our intuitive wisdom. I feel my Grandmother Lidia has never stopped being my caregiver, my godmother and my teacher. She continues to be my spiritual guide, ever present in good times and bad.

This is the time when we must awaken to our truth. The time is ripe to declare love boldly and fearlessly. Now is the time to forgive those we feel have injured us and to ask forgiveness from those we have wronged. Life is an eternal demonstration of awareness. We must, therefore, give thanks for the ability to be aware of even a single precious thought. If we are to be aware of anything, let that single thought be the recognition of our relationship to ourselves and to the world we inhabit. This is the time to awaken to our deep inner truth and to live our lives fully awake.

Choosing to Forgive

Every second of our lives we have an opportunity to choose. In fact, our life can be defined as a sum total of the decisions and choices we have made and their subsequent outcomes. With every thought, we have a choice, an opportunity to either think the best or the worst of any given situation. For example, as you are on your way to a party, you can tell yourself that the event will be exciting and you can be filled with anticipation. On the other hand, you can just as easily tell yourself that the event will be boring, filled with people you don't want to see. Suddenly, you can regret having to go at all. Either way, when you get to the event, people will be able to tell how you feel about being there because you will project outwardly what you are thinking internally. Your every thought gets out before you and it announces to people how you are feeling. Your thoughts betray you through your body language, providing great insight into your perception of life, yourself and others.

Now that you have identified what is troublesome and limiting, you must learn to release and let go. Letting go means having to learn to forgive. To forgive does not mean that you have to ignore the pain and suffering you endured. Forgiveness doesn't make you a martyr or glutton for punishment. When you forgive, you let go of the negative feelings *YOU* have been har-boring because someone else harmed you. Often, the person who harmed you may not be affected at all. They may not be aware of the level of harm they inflicted. They may not care, or they may not even be alive any more. Yet, you are still holding on to your pain and suffering.

Often times, forgiveness can be difficult because we tend to allow our pain and suffering to define who we are. We hold on to resentment and pain because we expect that someone will be outraged by our suffering and the injustice we experienced. We want someone to ask us for forgiveness, or make things right, or love us, or... Meanwhile, as we hold on to our resentment, we stop growing and become guarded and closed to new experiences and relationships.

Forgiveness must be an active decision to let go of pain and suffering...for your OWN sake. We must be aware of our choice to forgive and let go, knowing that resentment and bitterness become heavy burdens that limit our ability to soar. By choosing to forgive and let go, you release pent up energy that can be used in more productive ways to increase your joy and success.

What do you have to release? What are the held resentments, the pain and suffering to which you've held on. Can you choose to release the pain and all those situations and individuals you've held responsible for your restricted existence? If you choose to release and let go, you will discover that nothing you have ever suffered has limited you in anyway. You are as whole and complete today as you have ever been. Releasing and letting go of your held resentments will also release vast amounts of energy that you can apply to AWAKEN to full freedom and joy.

Day Five

**Task: RELEASE- Learning to Forgive...
and actually LET GO of the resentments**

AFFIRMATION

Theme: The Pathway to Transformation

There is a clear path that opens before me and transforms my life. I have participated in carving this path with my faith and my daily practice. The path appears before me clear and unhindered and I commit to follow it with unwavering confidence. I am not bound by the past. I release all attachment to resentment and guilt. I forgive those that have knowingly or unknowingly hurt me. As I forgive, I feel the weight of my load diminishing. My thoughts, my words and my actions are unified and represent the manifestation of my vision and my soul's deepest desires. I believe in the eternal promise which states, "All those who seek shall find." As I walk on this path I am able to decipher clues that reveal the greatness that unfolds before me. I am vigilant and remain alert, knowing that the creative spirit is always searching to communicate through everyone I meet and everything I see. I commit myself fully to this path, knowing that the journey is eternal and that nothing can impede my divine inheritance. Each step I take brings me closer to the truth of my most profound reality and I am able to see myself as a perfect embodiment of divine power and love. I know, beyond any shadow of doubt, that the light that burns within me is the light of all creation.

2. MEDITATION

3. JOURNALING EXERCISE

The theme for today's journal entries is **Release**.

1. Make a list of all the people who have wronged you, going back as far as you can. Describe the incident and what exactly they did. Then, most importantly, write down HOW THAT MADE YOU FEEL?

2. Do you see any similarities in their personality traits or characteristics?

3. What are the factors that have kept you from being able to forgive and let go?

4. What do you need to see or experience before you are able to let go?

5. What do you feel has been the cost of holding on to your pain?

6. Now, make a list of the people you've wronged. Again, go back as far as you can, remembering particularly the incidents you are most ashamed of.

7. Do you see any similarities in these incidents you have written down? Were some of them related to certain feelings that regularly crop up in you, such as anger, jealousy, bitterness, resentment, rage, sorrow, or fear?

8. Do you begin to see similarities in your triggers?

  a. Seeing patterns in our own behavior is the sign of some deeper operating belief inside. Once we see the patterns, we can identify the operating belief. Once we identify the belief we can ask ourselves the simple questions, "Do I want to keep this belief anymore? Does this core belief reflect who I really am?"

9. What does it feel like to remember these people and incidents?

10. Write down how it likely made each person feel when you wronged him or her.

11. Can you now say, "I forgive myself for hurting this person. I release my sorrow and guilt"?

8

DAY 6: ASSESS:
MEASURING YOUR PROGRESS

"Todo cabe en un jarrito sabiéndolo acomodar."[31]

...Grandmother Lidia

In the early 1970's, when my parents immigrated to the United States, Mexico had experienced an intense drop in its economy and a severe devaluation of the peso. My father lost all he had worked hard to build, his little grocery store and farm were a total ruin and he was broke and scared. Although he had been in the United States as a farm worker when he was a young man, now, as a husband and father of six children, my father felt he had failed. He was ashamed that my mother had to work in a factory to help care for the home and he saw it as a personal

---

31   *"Everything fits in a little jar, if you know how to place it right."*
There is a proper place for everything. We need not worry about what appears to be impossible. Step by step, things will fall into place.

failure. Soon, my father started to medicate himself by drinking to the point of oblivion. He drank to escape and he escaped all the time.

Today, I understand that my moving to California, over a decade ago, was an attempt to understand and connect to my absent and alcoholic father by retracing his footsteps. Maybe through my close connection with my grandmother we were both trying to heal our own respective relationship with my father. Perhaps through me, my grandmother was seeking my father's forgiveness and his salvation and perhaps I wanted to understand my father better by being close to his mother. In any case, I now know that I have tried to understand myself by understanding my father and I have tried to find myself by retracing my father's footsteps.

I didn't know anyone in California, but the Golden State appealed to me in many ways. California, after all, represents the ancestral mythical lands where Huichilopotzli's grandfather and other Toltec and Aztec gods were born. Northern California is the land of Aztlan, the ancestral home that gave birth to the vision of Tenochtitlan. When gold was discovered, California became a foreign land but the echoes of the ancestral spirits never stopped whispering their eternal wisdom. My father and grandfather had worked many years in the fields and farms of northern California, enriching its rich soil with their sweat.

When I was a child, my father kept repeating that he wanted us to get an education so that we would not have to work with our hands the way he had to.

"Only animals should have to work with
the strength of their backs.

Don't be like me.

You learn to work with your head
and not with your hands,"

My father would often say to me.

I was to experience California as my father's son, contributing in my own way to enriching the ancestral land by learning to work with my head and not my hands and hoping in the process to earn my father's pride.

Since my childhood, since the times when I watched my grandmother prepare her remedies, my life had been set in motion. Watching my grandmother work and hearing her stories I now know that I was being prepared to be a healer even when I had no awareness of the preparations being made.

I have been trained as a healer in two separate traditions. I obtained my doctorate in the healing profession of Clinical Psychology in a traditional academic institution. However, I was also taught by my Grandmother Lidia, who, as I've mentioned, was a *Curandera*.[32] As the oldest son of her oldest son, I was her first grandson, her godson and her willing student.

I have always found that my grandmother's teachings preserve a profound truth that continues to reveal itself in every aspect of my life. Finding my unique voice by honoring both my traditional psychological training and my ancestral heritage has been my greatest challenge, motivation and reward in life.

As I embarked on my journey, many years ago, I was opening my heart and mind and allowing myself to be guided by the transformative power of my ancestors flowing through me. As the oldest son of Grandmother Lidia's oldest son, I had been chosen. My destiny has been to find some way of honoring my grandmother's entrusted teachings and honor the legacy of fierce love that would forge our future families with pride and the inner Awareness that we are children of the Creator.

"El hombre impone y dios dispone."[33]

...Grandmother Lidia

Throughout my life, my Grandmother Lidia's teachings and her influence reminded me of the existence of a universe

---

32 Mexican folk healer.
33 *"Man imposes and God disposes."* We may be imposed upon by man-made laws, and we may spend our days imposing our will and wishes on life, constantly planning and scheming. Yet, the greater mind of God determines ultimate outcome.

governed by invisible forces. She taught me that reality is not the material manifestation. It is not the world that we control and manipulate. The source of truth and power lies in understanding the force and spirit that brings all matter and life into a manifested reality. There are creative and generative laws to use at our disposal. These divine laws and principles demand respect, deep knowing and congruency. These laws always operate the same for everyone. Those that believe and follow will be rewarded with what is manifested in their lives. You have chosen to embark upon this eternal journey of self-discovery. You have signed up to confirm that transmutation is not only possible, but our very purpose for being. What is transmutation? The process by which – through fire and purification – a lesser material transforms itself into something greater, purer than its previous self. You have entered into your sixth day of AWAKENING.

Day Six

Task: ASSESS-Measuring your Progress

AFFIRMATION

Theme: Celebrating the Glory of Your Higher Self

Light breaks through the darkness. The loving hand of Creation taps at my door with an unmistakable and persistent knocking I cannot ignore. I know that the highest mental practice I can engage in is to listen to this force that has deemed me worthy of such invitation. I see my good manifesting before me and I give thanks as I recognize my awakening. I constantly look for the progress that I have made and I reward myself, knowing that such self-recognition will bring greater manifestations. Without a trace of fear and with complete certainty and faith, I release all attachment to my limiting past. I know that the light that has illuminated saints, masters and sages in the past is the same light that burns within me today. I know that there is but one life and one perfect activity. This one life and activity is always operating out of love and compassion. I therefore, release all my past attachments to pain, grief and loss. I remove all barriers to my experience of good, knowing that the spirit of creation can never be exhausted. I know that this eternal spirit is the same spirit that lives within me. Every day of my life, I AWAKEN to a higher realization of love and a more profound awareness of my true self.

1. MEDITATION

2. JOURNALING EXERCISE

In the beginning of this book, you were asked to write out your life story. You set some bench marks on a Likert Scale that asked you to rate yourself on various categories. Well, it's time for you to assess your current status on those same measures.

Today, your life story asks you to ASSESS. You do this by going back through the exact same questions asked in the first chapter, re-asking them using the Likert Scale as your mechanism for gauging where you are at. Answer the questions to respond to your current status. Go through each of the numbered questions and select a number from one to ten that best describes your current assessment. The questions beginning with a letter are once again to be answered in your journal. Many of your responses may be similar, but you should also begin to see changes in your responses as your consciousness has begun to shift, since you began your exercises and Week of Awakening.

Part 1: Post-test

1—2—3—4—5—6—7—8—9—10

Least/Little   Much/Most

Assessment Questions:

1. Do I care for my mind?

A. In what ways can I better care for my mind?

2. Do I care for my body?

A. In what ways can I better care for my body?

3. **Do I care for my spirit?**

    A. In what ways can I better care for my spirit – my sense of self-love?

4. **Am I content and joyful for my life as it is right now?**

    A. What is one small change I would love to permanently make to my life?

    B. What is the biggest thing in my life that I wish to change?

    C. What are the 10 things, people, places, or experiences I know I do NOT want in my life anymore? In other words, what are the sources of negative energy in my life that I know I must remove, or push away from, if I am ever going to discover my happiness?

5. **Am I certain that I am living my unique purpose and to my potential?**

    A. What do I believe my true life purpose is?

    B. If I don't know, what MIGHT it be? What are three things I've often thought would bring me great joy to be doing more of?

    C. What would bring me the greatest joy to be doing with my life?

    D. Do I have the courage to begin a new life doing what I love?

6. **Do I know what I need in order to make the necessary changes in my life?**

    A. What are these things I need to have or do
       or speak in order to change my life, NOW?

7. Rather than sitting and waiting for change to take place, am I doing what I can to implement the changes I wish to see?

    A. If not, why not?

    B. What am I most afraid of?

    C. Do I have the courage to pass through my fear? Do I want a NEW life and NEW joy badly enough to be willing to push through my fears, even though my knees may be shaking?

Part 2:

Once you have completed your week of journaling, you will leave your journal alone for a few days and then go back and re-read your journal entries. Go back to the start of your journal when you first answered these same questions. Compare the ratings that you gave yourself at the beginning with the number rating that you are giving yourself at the end. What changed? How much change did you experience? Are there any surprises? Journal your responses to these questions. Here are a few more questions for you to think about, ruminate on, and also write out and answer in your journal.

1. What are your scores today?

2. How much work have you completed in the previous six days?

3. How much have you applied yourself?

4. What have you discovered about yourself?

As you compare your scores for today with your initial assessment, your scores matter, but what matters even more is how you grade yourself.

1. Are you a strict evaluator? A hard critic?

2. Are you focusing on what you didn't accomplish or are you in celebration and recognition of what you've shown yourself?

How you see your progress or lack thereof says a great deal about your current level of AWAKENING. Take inventory. Let your inventory be generous and sincere.

1. Do you see who you really are? Are you beginning to?

2. Can you appreciate all of the work you have done in order to get yourself to this place?

3. What do you feel?

4. How do your feelings differ today from what you felt before you started this process?

5. Do you see how much you have grown?

Coming to Greater Aliveness...Finally

Now, don't you see that a sudden AWAKENING is not only possible, it is inevitable! It is your divine destiny. AWAKENING to the light of a new awareness that screams to you:

"You are eternal and powerful!"

You have the ability to liberate yourself and to recreate yourself into the person you were always intended to be. Rise up from your bended knee. Sacrifice yourselves no further. It is time to collect on the promise. It is time to ask for the fruits of the labor and convert the sweat from the fields into the rain of gold. We have AWAKENED from our slumber and we are recalling that we are so much more than the flesh and blood that is our vehicle. We are spirits embodied having an awareness of our experience as we unfold from the depths of desire and despair to be uplifted in our recognition of unity with the vital source of all goodness and love.

Are you Awakening? Is your life changing in the direction of your soul's desire? The best person to judge whether you are changing or not, has got to be yourself. Only you truly know you. Only you can hear your inner voice. Only you can give yourself permission to become who you truly are.

Are you finally ready to come ALIVE?

9

DAY 7: GRATITUDE: REWARD YOURSELF AND CELEBRATE YOUR ACCOMPLISHMENTS

"Cántale a la vida si quieres que la vida te cante." [34]

...Grandmother Lidia

The life we have constructed is a summary of our past experiences, thoughts and actions. These memories, thoughts and behaviors are fleeting and fluid, yet more and more, we are learning that our physical environment responds to our mental activity. If you are holding on to a great deal of pain, suffering and mistrust, you are manifesting a life that reinforces your limiting beliefs, but your limiting beliefs can be corrected and realigned with the eternal truth that resides within you.

---

34 *"Sing to life, and life will sing to you."* Remaining grateful and joy-filled creates a reflective reaction from life, only increasing your joy.

If you begin to analyze your life, you will likely be able to identify unhealthy thoughts and behavior patterns. You will be able to see how these thoughts and behaviors have limited and negatively impacted your life. You will be able to create a plan of action to incorporate new thoughts and behaviors and you will begin to witness the changes that take place around you. You can learn a new way of being at a pace that is easy for you to digest. Your AWAKENING is a life time commitment and the more you discover about yourself, the more powerful you will become.

More than you can imagine, the physical world bends and organizes itself to correspond with your thoughts. We are directing the very basic elements of creation with the power of our thoughts. We are constantly inviting experiences into our field of perception simply with the power of our word and thought. In the beginning was the thought and the thought became the word and the word became manifested. We are in an eternal dance of manifestation and we are lovingly lead to discover greater and purer expressions of our true identities as sons and daughters of a new sun. If we are awake to the lessons life presents, we grow and become more joyful and powerful. We are the divine heirs to the riches of the unbound. We have put our hand out, asking for what we believe is our divine heritage. The answer to the request has always been, "YES!" Most often, what we have come to receive is far greater than what we have requested.

It is never too late to reconstruct our lives. If we are going through life asleep and unaware we can continue to make the necessary changes in our thoughts and behaviors to become more aware and to manifest the life we deeply desire. We can begin to recognize that our thoughts and our words are so powerful that they can materialize themselves right before our very eyes. If we nurture a thought and hold on to that vision, it will eventually become a reality. The Universal Law of creation always proves that this is so. Those thoughts you entertained yesterday, have become the physical, manifested reality of your world today. If you hold on to a limited memory of pain, fear or suffering, this experience creates the perspective through which you come to view reality. An AWAKENING provides you with a sudden realization that what you thought was true, is not. You might have held resentments towards your mother for not giving you the love you needed, until one day you discover that your mother's parents used to beat her and often left her alone feeling unwanted when she was a child. This new insight can cause you to have a different perspective about life, inevitably changing not just your relationship to your mother, but your very notion of your own self. You leave the anger behind and you are more AWAKENED and open.

In order for these AWAKENINGS to create true change, you have to integrate them and make them part of your daily life. Sometimes, discovering so much new information can make your head spin and leave you fearful and overwhelmed. Scared, you may start to resist your transformation, wondering how much of your old self to retain and how much of the new awareness to integrate.

As humans, we are evolving faster than ever. Our notion of time is changing also. The bombardment of information and constant stimulation makes time seem to move faster. Indeed, our ancestors predicted these times of transition. They requested of us, their descendants, the Children of the Fifth Sun, that we never to forget our true origin.

> *"Nunca olvides de dónde vienes y quien eres.*
> *Aunque muchas sean las tentaciones del deseo,*
> *solo te enriquece lo que refleja tu verdad."* 35

...Grandmother Lidia

We are the survivors of conquests and wars, of oppressive thieves and corrupted governments. We have endured predatory institutions and unjust laws and still we are ever rising and evolving. Now is our ultimate evolution and final revolution. When we join our thought and action to the principles and laws of the unified Creative force, we recognize ourselves as one with this power. In this recognition we see there is nothing to fear, nothing that can ever limit us permanently. We are forever free and forever unbound. This is the age of AWAKENING. It is time

---

35 *"Never forget where you came from and who you are. Although many may be the temptations of desire, you are enriched only by what reflects your truth."*

to shed the limited, fear-based identity you previously adopted as your personality and embrace your TRUE SELF.

Stay open and unafraid. Sometimes, what you will discover along the way can make you feel small and remorseful, but don't linger too long in these feelings of regret and self-pity. There is too much work to be done. Instead, when you come into a higher awareness of yourself, lift your head in gratitude and praise because you have recognized that you are leaving behind a lesser version of who you once were.

Be prepared! If you start to desire to gain a deeper sense of yourself, you will! Be ready to let go of the past and embrace your new SELF. As I was preparing to finish this book, I was aware of the drastic and transformative changes happening in my own life. The more I thought and wrote, the more drastic the changes occurred around me. I had been working on a draft of this book for several months and had come to that precious moment in a writer's life when the end of the book becomes visible. As I looked over the draft, I began to ask myself how I could prove that this program actually works. I realized that I had been living this program much of my life, since that fateful day I fell asleep.

The changes I have witnessed in my life have been so powerful that I am now happier than I have ever been. I have greater success than I could have imagined, and in unusual ways. Joyfully, I am no longer fearfully attached to the trappings of success or the lure of accumulating things simply to possess. I have found financial, emotional and spiritual freedom. Even as abundance continues to flow into my life, I am increasingly more appreciative and grateful for the uncomplicated, simple joys of life. The rise of a new sun brings me the opportunity to celebrate creation once again. A look into my beloved's eyes and the very gates of heaven are open to me. Every day brings with it new adventures and surprises, promises of rewards greater than those I imagined yesterday. Perhaps the greatest of all rewards is knowing that the source of AWAKENING is never exhausted. As much as I am given and as fortunate as I become, I could never even slightly diminish the unbound generosity that is always available.

Rewarding Yourself

It is most important to reward yourself each time you catch yourself having incorporated new behaviors or changed from old patterns of thinking. You have reached an incredible point in your life. In essence, you have unlocked the secret code to your personality and can now change thoughts and behaviors you have determined do not serve you. This is a huge achievement and you deserve to celebrate your accomplishments. Rewarding yourself in some fashion, even if it is just recognizing your progress and patting yourself on the back, is an important part of the transformative process. Gratitude gives your mind a sense of direction by providing an image, or road map to what you want. The mind holds on to the experience of pleasure and success and sets out to duplicate that experience.

You have now completed the seven steps in the transformative process.

1. You have learned to identify a problem. (Awareness)

2. You have identified the source and nature of that problem. (Identification)

3. You have interrupted the limiting thoughts and/or behaviors that maintain the repetitive patterns. (Interruption)

4. You've learned to incorporate new thoughts and behaviors. (Incorporation)

5. You've learned to release resentments and hostilities. (Release)

6. You've learned to conduct a self-assessment and track your growth. (Assessment)

7. Perhaps most importantly, you've learned to remain grateful and reward yourself when you've done some great work. (Reward)

You have successfully learned how to adopt a new behavior and to replace the old. Give yourself the verbal praise and recognition you deserve. Catch yourself practicing new behaviors. Notice the difference in your body and in your thoughts. Affirm your new thoughts and behaviors. Tell yourself how this new adaptation is so much healthier for your life. By rewarding yourself you are increasing your ability to learn quicker and more effectively. You are instructing your mind to seek new experiences and you are increasing your ability to integrate new changes with growing ease and comfort.

What do you use to reward yourself? How often are you aware of your need to reward yourself?

Day Seven

Task: REWARD YOURSELF-
Celebrate Your Accomplishments

1. AFFIRMATION

Theme: Reflection and Inner Peace

I sit in the stillness and peace that I find at the center of my soul. I bask in the glow and warmth of this embrace. I am able to feel the sacred silence that surrounds me. I feel a deep sense of peace and an undeniable power stir within me. I gladly give myself over to this loving presence. I surrender all that I have been, knowing that no past mistake, no past experience can harm me or limit me in any way. My mind, heart and soul are open to receive all the blessings that are rightfully mine. I declare that I am a worthy and deserving child of creation. I see the doors to the eternal treasures opening before me. As I let go, I am at once connected to all that has ever been and all that will ever be. I am able to direct this loving force to create the life intended for me. My heart and mind are purified and all thoughts of doubt and limitation are removed, revealing the essence of my true self. I surrender and sacrifice the old 'me' that was full of doubt and uncertainty and I awaken to the great divine reality within me. My true self reaches beyond the limits of space and time and I bask in the recognition of my true and divine eternal nature.

2. MEDITATION

3. JOURNALING EXERCISE

Part 1: Creating a Plan of Action

Congratulations, you have completed this week of Awakening. During this process, you have obtained the necessary skills to change unhealthy thought and behavior patterns with those that are more congruent with your intended path. After the week is complete choose one day to review your journal entries and notes.

You have completed a great deal of work. You wrote down your life story and you identified patterns of thoughts and behaviors that have repeated themselves in your life. You've gotten some insight as to the fears, wants and needs that have kept your patterns active. Now it's time to take a look at your journal entries. Read your journal entries for each day as if you were reading a book someone else wrote. Try to keep your emotional reactions in check. It is important to adopt the attitude of an objective observer. In other words, read your journal entries as if you were reading someone else's life story.

Again, see if you can identify any negative thought or behavior patterns. Spend some time writing these unhealthy thought and behavior patterns down to examine them closer.

Try to describe these patterns in as much detail as you can. How did the patterns begin? How were these patterns reinforced? How and when did these patterns become limiting in your growth and further development?

As you read your description and narrative regarding your top three emerging patterns answer the following questions for each of the identified patterns:

1. Of the patterns that you have already identified, are any of these patterns a surprise to you?

2. When and how did you first become aware that you were being limited by this pattern of thoughts and/or behaviors?

3. What have you identified as the main problem in this pattern of thought and/or behavior?

4. How do you plan to interrupt the typical and useful way you have reacted to this pattern in the past?

5. What new behavior or thought will you use to alter the usual way that you have reacted in the past?

6. How will you mark the release of the old limiting pattern?

7. What measures or benchmarks will you use
   to show how you have changed?

8. How do you intend to reward yourself for the
   progress that you have made?

Answer the questions above for each of the limiting patterns
that you have identified and analyze your responses. Your answer
to the questions above represent your plan of action. By answering
the questions and following through on your identified actions
steps, you will be able to alter any fixed patterns of thoughts or
behaviors that have previously limited your growth. Changing
thoughts may require constant observation and attention, but
the rewards will soon be evident in your happier life.

Some of us have trouble rewarding ourselves. We tend to
do for others and leave ourselves for last or we simply never get
around to satisfying our own needs and wants. As long as others
are taken care of, we are fine, or so we think. This attitude sends
a message to your mind that you are not important and your
needs do not matter.

Your needs may rise up as a thought, but if you don't pay
attention to your needs, they tend to fall to the back of your
thoughts until you can't hear your own needs anymore. The
result is that you build self-resentment. By paying attention
to your needs and rewarding your efforts, you are not only
emphasizing that you matter, but you are directing your mind
to continue to work hard because your hard work is recognized
and rewarded by the person that matters most, YOU. This

self-reward, thus, has the effect of increasing targeted and desired behaviors in the future.

- What else can you learn by reading your journal entries?

- What feelings do you experience as you review these patterns?

Now, select the top three thought and/or behavior patterns which are most troublesome or most pressing for you. Write these down on a separate sheet of paper so that they are listed all by themselves. Do you see any theme evident in the top three thought and/or behavior patterns you identified? The top three patterns you've identified signify the areas in your life in which you need to focus your efforts for change and liberation.

1. What actions will you commit to implement?

2. What time frame are you giving yourself to assess your progress.

3. What are the measures or benchmarks that you will use to determine your progress.

4. What rewards will you give yourself?

5. When you get stuck, how will you keep yourself on task and how will you reduce the negative talk that can sabotage your progress?

Setting Goals and Objectives

You will now create a plan of action to address these patterns. Start by clearly stating your goal at the top of the page. Your goal should be simple and clearly stated and easily measurable. If, for example, you choose to lose weight to feel better, you might state this as a goal. "I will lose ten pounds in two months." This is a simple, do-able goal, stated in clear and measurable fashion. Now, under your goal write down three objectives. Your goal statement declares the outcome you want to achieve. The objectives then outline the necessary steps to achieve your goal. For your goal of losing weight, one objective might be that during the next two months, you will reduce your calorie intake and eliminate foods that are high in fat. A second objective might be that you will exercise at least three times per week for no less than thirty minutes per day.

Do the same for the other goals that you have established, outlining measurable objectives checking your progress periodically. If you have to, modify your goals and objectives to more accurately reflect your progress.

Part 2: Rewarding Yourself

1. What are the things you can do to show that you are rewarding yourself?

2. What do you feel about the work that you completed during this week of awakening?

3. What have you learned about yourself?

4. What commitments are you making for yourself to continue your journey of awakening.

5. How do you intend to share your new awakenings and realizations with the world?

6. What are you eliminating from your life?

7. What is the greatest realization that you have made during this process?

10

UNBOUNDED AWAKENING: YOUR AWAKENING REPRESENTS THE RISING OF THE 5TH SUN

"Dios está en la tierra, en el cielo y en todo lugar,
pero más le gusta estar dentro de ti." [36]

…Grandmother Lidia

Human life has evolved over thousands of years. According to our ancestors, the evolution of life is also the evolution of human awareness, or 'consciousness.' Our native ancestors learned to record the past twenty-five thousand years of human existence. They organized the history of human evolution into five different periods, or 'worlds.' Each world, governed by its respective sun, came in and out of existence. These are the five stages of human evolution and the evolution of consciousness. In the final 'world' of enlightenment we recognize that the frail ego

---

36 *"God is on earth, in the heavens, and in every place. But He most enjoys being within you."*

falls away and we join with the whole of creation, recognizing that all the barriers and limitations are forever removed. We are the mind of God aware of him-/herself.

It is said that we live in the fifth and final period governed by the Fifth Sun. This is the final and ultimate evolution. This is the time when humanity must be open to the evolution of consciousness and awareness. Science and spirituality are coming together in a recognition that we as humans are co-creators of our reality. We have the power to orchestrate and command the universal forces and these forces must respond to our command. With such power at our disposal how can we not choose to liberate ourselves from fear, uncertainty and limitation? When you learn to rely on the wakening within, you will be illuminated by a heightened awareness. A new sun will rise within you and you will see that you hold the power to orchestrate matter into existence.

I've come to appreciate every decision and effort that has been necessary to bring me to this moment in life. Nothing has been wasted. My suffering and fear have pushed me and propelled me to keep moving forward and keep reaching higher. For years, I strived to understand the reasons why certain things happened, and I resisted accepting things that I simply could not change.

I have tested love and I have tested my Creator. Each time, I have been delivered and made stronger. Today, I don't need to test. I KNOW! Beyond any shadow of doubt, I know that I am strong – a survivor who is a blessing and a healing presence to those I encounter!

I have often thought greatly of myself and barely about others. I have felt needy and have feared being abandoned. I've grown proud and arrogant and have allowed my lower drives to lead me into dead ends that have wounded my body and tested my will to survive, but I have endured. Throughout my experiences I have learned that life does not have to be lived as a constant re-injury.

I dare to let go of all that has kept me down and in the dark. I rise to my potential by breaking free from the endless repetition of patterns that only served to oppress me. Today, I am focused on generating greater good for myself and those that I love. I am excited to create family and community wherever I go. I am a source of healing and support to all those that I encounter and I am in turn renewed and enriched by my friendships. My life is truly limitless and so is yours.

We have entered into the age of co-creation. This is the era of self-discovery that was foretold for thousands of years by our ancestors. We are realizing that we are forever creating our own reality and capable of altering it to correspond to our ever-evolving and expanded consciousness. We release the hold we've had on our previous identity.

This book has been written in order to give you the basic, necessary tools needed to release and remove any and all barriers to your full potential. By learning to break limiting patterns of thought and behavior you have taken control of your life and you've learned to move in the direction of the creative force that surrounds you. By releasing your attachments to past suffering and limitation, you've learned to reconstruct your life to fit your unique purpose. Now that you have completed this seven day program, I suggest you take a break and try to pay attention to your new environment. See the world with your new eyes and learn to perceive with your new senses. I encourage you to, periodically, pick up the book again and repeat the seven-day program in a future time when you feel the need to recommit.

Welcome to your AWAKENED self. Your transformation has been awaited. You are the essential ingredient required for the transformation of our entire planet.

APPENDIX

Affirmations from The Promise of the Fifth Sun (as composed and compiled by Da'Mon Vann)

Feel free to incorporate these one-line affirmations into your morning and evening meditations and/or carry it with you during the day as a reminder and mantra when you catch your thoughts slipping into negative patterns.

1. I choose to believe that I am an active participant in the creation of the life I live.

2. My thoughts reproduce and become manifest in the body as energy and behavior.

3. My mind is fertile ground. I hold guard over my thoughts. Whatever seeds I plant are the seeds I will harvest.

4. I am constantly vigilant and present to the choices I make every second of my life.

5. My mind has boundless creative energy and it has the power to construct according to my devotion and will. I thoughtfully guide and direct this power to...

6. Above all, I learn to be gentle with myself and I reward myself when I identify patterns of thought that previously harmed me. I release, let go and embrace my heightened sense of awareness.

7. I learn to let go of hate and release those that I have held responsible for my hatred. I write a better story of my past and I become actively involved in the creation of my improved reality.

8. I am deserving of all the goodness of life.

9. My thoughts have the power to manifest a better world.

10. I face my past with courage and gratitude. No matter how troubling my past has been, I choose to move forward with grace into a greater day. I allow peace and joy to enter my present life.

11. My existence is essential. The universe awaits my contribution...(to the continuing saga of our human evolution.)

12. I know that no obstacle can obstruct my inherited divine destiny. I know that I am capable of greatness.

13. I dare to imagine that anything is possible in my life. The world is limited only by my perception. I expand the capacity of my mind to think beyond what I believe is possible.

14. I hold my desires as a constant in my mind without concern for how such desires will come true. I keep watch over my thoughts and any appearances to the contrary.

15. I am the legacy of the past and the creator of my future. I was intended to be free, to live in joy and prosperity.

16. At my core, I am as complete today as I was the day I was born. I have everything I need to live beyond fear and limitation.

17. My thoughts are creative energy. The source and potential of my thoughts are unlimited and can be directed. I learn to stop the automatic negative thinking.

18. The power of my thoughts manifests everything that is matter and material in my world.

19. As all things begin with the power of thought, I know that there can be no such thing as an external enemy unless, I conceive of one as such.

20. I move with the rhythm of life. I maintain a flexible mind in order to continue to grow. I choose to make life as rich as I dare imagine. I desire to be happy and free.

21. I listen and honor that inner wisdom in my mind. In doing so, I discover the healing, ancestral source of all goodness and truth; my true nature.

22. I quiet my mind in moments of uncertainty and hear the voice of truth, which reveals that everything is alright right where I am!

23. I appreciate the perfection and simplicity of each moment just as it is. I see beyond the confusion of my individual reality.

CPSIA information can be obtained
at www.ICGtesting.com
Printed in the USA
FFOW04n1242020517
35222FF